In Search of Being

IN SEARCH of BEING

The Fourth Way to Consciousness

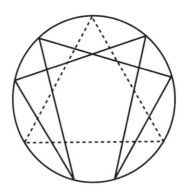

G. I. Gurdjieff

SHAMBHALA
Boston & London
2012

Shambhala Publications, Inc.
Horticultural Hall
300 Massachusetts Avenue
Boston, Massachusetts 02115
www.shambhala.com

9 8 7 6 5 4 3 2 1

First Edition
Printed in the United States of America

♾ This edition is printed on acid-free paper that meets
the American National Standards Institute z39.48 Standard.
♻ This book was printed on 30% postconsumer
recycled paper. For more information please visit
www.shambhala.com.

Distributed in the United States by Random House, Inc.,
and in Canada by Random House of Canada Ltd

Library of Congress Cataloging-in-Publication Data
Gurdjieff, Georges Ivanovitch, 1872–1949.
In search of being: the fourth way to consciousness / G.I. Gurdjieff.—1st ed.
p. cm.
Includes bibliographical references and index.
ISBN 978-1-61180-037-1 (hardcover: alk. paper)
1. Fourth Way (Occultism) 2. Self-consciousness (Awareness)
3. Awareness. I. Title.
BP605.G815 2012
197—dc23
2012026373

Contents

Foreword

ONE HUNDRED YEARS AGO in Russia, George Ivanovitch Gurdjieff (1866–1949) introduced an ancient teaching of man's conscious evolution, a forgotten science for perceiving reality in oneself and in the universe. Although he was virtually unknown during his lifetime, in the years after his death Gurdjieff's ideas have spread throughout the world, inspiring new generations of seekers to explore the esoteric meaning of traditional religions. Up to now, however, his early teaching has been reproduced only in fragments of talks from 1915 to 1924, arranged in chronological order; no attempt has been made to present this teaching in his own words as a comprehensive whole.

Gurdjieff regarded knowledge of reality—what he called true "knowledge of being"—as a stream flowing from remote antiquity, passed down from age to age, from people to people, from race to race. He viewed this knowledge as the indispensable means to achieve inner liberation. For those seeking to understand the meaning of human life in the universe, he said, the aim of the search is to break through to this stream, to find it. Then there remains only *to know* in order *to be*. But in order to know, he taught, it is necessary to find out "how to know."

Gurdjieff respected traditional paths toward spiritual transformation, and pointed out that their different approaches could be subsumed under one of three categories: the "way of the fakir," which centers on mastery of the physical body; the "way of the monk," based on faith and religious feeling; and the "way of the yogi," which concentrates on developing the mind. He presented his teaching as a "Fourth Way" that requires work on all three aspects at the same time. Instead of obedience or faith, this way calls for knowing and understanding—the awakening of another intelligence. His personal wish, he once said, was to live and teach so that there should be a new conception of God in the world, a change in the very meaning of the word.

Born in 1866 in the Caucasus on the frontier of Russia and Turkey, from childhood Gurdjieff felt he had to understand the mystery of human existence, and delved deeply into religion and science to find some explanation. He found both approaches persuasive and consistent within themselves, but bound to reach contradictory conclusions, given the different premises from which they began. He became convinced that separately neither religion nor science could explain the meaning of human life. At the same time, Gurdjieff felt certain that a real and complete knowledge had existed in ancient times, and must have been handed down orally from generation to generation in various civilizations. He set out to find those who had this knowledge, traveling over a period of some twenty years. His journeys extended from Greece and Egypt to Central Asia, including the mountains of the Hindu Kush and Tibet.

With a small team of comrades, Gurdjieff found and put together elements of a forgotten knowledge that reconciled the great traditional beliefs. He called it "ancient science" but did not identify its origin or those who discovered it. This science viewed the world of visible matter as modern physics does, recognizing the equivalence of mass and energy, the subjective illusion of time, the general theory of relativity. But its inquiry did not stop there, accepting as real only phenomena that could be measured and proven by controlled experiment. This science also explored the mystic's world outside sense perception, the vision of another reality, infinite beyond space and time. The aim was to understand the place of man in the cosmic order, the meaning of human life on the earth, and actually to know and experience in oneself the reality of both finite and infinite worlds at the same time. This science originated in civilizations in Central Asia and Egypt, and its principles were incorporated in all the traditional religions. Gurdjieff said it could be called "esoteric Christianity," but noted these principles were developed thousands of years before Jesus Christ. It could also be called "esoteric Buddhism," with its origin thousands of years before Gautama Buddha.

In 1912 Gurdjieff began to gather followers in Moscow and in 1915 organized a study group in St. Petersburg. Two years later, to escape the violence of the Russian Revolution, he moved to the Caucasus and eventually, in 1922, settled in France, where he established an institute to practice his teaching at the Château du Prieuré in Fontainebleau near Paris.

As described in the biographical notes at the back of this book, the leading figure in the appearance of the Fourth Way was P. D. Ouspensky, who joined Gurdjieff's group in 1915 and went with him to the Caucasus. Ouspensky was no ordinary follower. Endowed with a far-ranging mind and keen intellect, he had traveled widely as a journalist investigating theosophical and other esoteric traditions. From his own experiences he was convinced of the possibility of higher consciousness. After failing to contact an esoteric "school" in India, he was seeking the hidden knowledge that Gurdjieff and his comrades had discovered. As a writer and lecturer, he was the ideal recruit to receive the teaching and promote the Fourth Way.

When he first met Gurdjieff, Ouspensky was immediately interested to learn what Gurdjieff knew about esotericism and "schools" that taught it. He liked Gurdjieff's clear and precise manner of speaking and, true to his journalistic profession, kept notes that recorded Gurdjieff's exact words, often in entire pages of quoted remarks. After helping Gurdjieff form a group in St. Petersburg, over a period of eighteen months, Ouspensky pressed him to reveal, step by step, the basic elements of his ancient science, which the group called the "System." With Gurdjieff's permission, Ouspensky preserved his record of these talks and afterward arranged the material in an autobiographical manuscript entitled *Fragments of an Unknown Teaching*. In it he wrote that in

1921 he told Gurdjieff "in detail of a plan I had drawn up for a book to expound his St. Petersburg lectures. . . . He agreed to this plan."

For reasons set forth in the biographical notes, the book presenting the teaching was never written. Until 1924 Gurdjieff was busy with his institute in France, and then the writing of his magnum opus, *All and Everything*. Ouspensky established his own work in London, lecturing on the System and writing his book *A New Model of the Universe*. The separation between the two men precluded their collaboration. In fact, Ouspensky did not send Gurdjieff the manuscript of *Fragments* until 1947, the year of his own death. Gurdjieff confirmed its accuracy, and the manuscript was published posthumously in 1949 as Ouspensky's autobiographical account, even though over two-thirds consisted of verbatim quotations of Gurdjieff. (The French edition bore Ouspensky's title *Fragments d'un enseignement inconnu*, but the English title was changed to *In Search of the Miraculous* to avoid confusion with another author's book, *Fragments of a Faith Forgotten*, published the preceding year.)

The present book is intended to fulfill the original purpose for the St. Petersburg talks. It restates Gurdjieff's quoted exposition, supplemented by his later lectures, mostly in 1922–1924. These subsequent talks, which took place at the Prieuré in Fontainebleau and in New York, were recorded and arranged by Jeanne de Salzmann, Gurdjieff's closest follower. They were published in 1973 under the title *Views from the Real World*.

In Search of the Miraculous and *Views from the Real World* remain the authentic source books of Gurdjieff's early teaching. Ouspensky's autobiographical account vividly re-creates the adventure of his questioning, as well as his insights on critical aspects, including higher dimensions and interpreting the Enneagram. Both source books contain additional material on Gurdjieff's ideas about a variety of subjects, including education and art. In reconstructing his early teaching, this volume restates less than one-third of *In Search* and even less of *Views*, leaving the original sources as required reading for a complete picture of the teaching.

This book was arranged and edited with a small group of followers of Gurdjieff and of Mme. de Salzmann. Apart from this foreword

and the biographical notes, the text consists almost entirely of Gurdjieff's own words, restated from a new English translation of the original Russian text of *Fragments of an Unknown Teaching* and, with the
permission of Penguin Group (USA), from *Views from the Real World*.
The sole exception is the first subpart of chapter II ("Functions and
Centers"), which was derived from Ouspensky's *Psychology of Man's
Possible Evolution*, based on his representation that Gurdjieff explained
functions and centers "in the way they are set out in the psychological
lectures." Gurdjieff's spoken words, delivered at different times and
on different occasions, have been modified, mostly in style and voice,
where necessary for a consistent presentation in a single book. Care
has been taken to preserve Ouspensky's use of italics for emphasis,
and of quotation marks to signal conventional words having a special
meaning.

Readers approaching Gurdjieff's ideas for the first time should be
prepared for an iconoclastic challenge to the foundations of our modern worldview—specifically, man's consciousness and free will, progress and civilization, and the significance of human life in the universe.
Situating our solar system in the vastness of the Milky Way, the author
introduces the idea of scale in defining finite and infinite worlds. He
recalls the ancient theory of cosmoses and asserts that the fundamental laws governing phenomena are the same at all levels, that man is
a microcosm representing the whole universe. Thus reality is not to
be perceived by looking outside—a mystical vision of the earth or the
heavens—but by turning inward and seeing through time and space
within oneself. The ancient dictum "Know thyself" is invoked in its
original sense in the Egyptian Temple—a call to open to consciousness,
to see reality.

In the introduction, Gurdjieff dismisses modern, supposedly "scientific" knowledge as based on sense perception, and asserts that knowledge of reality can be learned only by a special kind of "self-study"
undertaken along with others. In the chapters that follow, he begins by
pointing out that realizing this possibility depends on our own wish and
effort; nobody else cares or can do this work for us. He then lays out the

principles of the teaching—but not as revealed truth to be believed or obeyed. On the contrary, the first principle is that nothing is to be taken on faith. The Fourth Way is, above all, one of *knowing*—not of belief or obedience. It is a *way of understanding*.

Gurdjieff offers this key advice for approaching his writing: "Do not take anything literally. Try simply to grasp the principle." This imperative obviously applies when he speaks of cosmic relationships (for example, the "ray of creation" or "food for the moon") or metaphysical concepts (acquiring transubstantial "bodies"). But it is equally applicable to his multibrain structure of human physiology, which he warns is proposed "only as a plan for one's self-observation." *Nothing should be taken literally.*

The biographical notes assume that the Fourth Way is an esoteric teaching of what Gurdjieff called Great Knowledge: the forgotten science of man's relation with God and the universe that was passed on to initiates over thousands of years in Central Asia, Egypt and Greece. It was his passion to discover this hidden knowledge that distinguished Gurdjieff's closest friend, a Russian prince and follower of Vajrayana Buddhism. And it was the principles of esoteric transmission that determined the respective roles of Gurdjieff and his closest followers, Ouspensky and Jeanne de Salzmann.

The definitive feature of esotericism is to differentiate between the outer, exoteric form of the teaching that is visible to the uninitiated and the inner, esoteric content that can be known only by adherents who practice it. The outer can be transmitted by a person who understands its doctrine, but the inner can be passed on only by an initiate who can, in practice, live the teaching. Gurdjieff makes this distinction in chapter V on religions when he differentiates between the teaching of doctrine specifying *what* is to be done and the teaching of practical knowledge of *how* to do it. For him, only a person who can live according to Christ's precepts has a right to call himself a Christian.

Gurdjieff's early teaching to the St. Petersburg group and at the Prieuré was in the outer form of ideas presented to people who had no experience in practical work for consciousness. Gurdjieff taught that the path to objective reality was through "self-consciousness," but could indicate the required direction only in conceptual terms, with illustrations from everyday experience. For example, the key relation among mind, feeling and body was expressed metaphorically in terms of the driver, horse and carriage. In analogizing to a house with four rooms, he referred to simultaneous "work" in the different rooms. And the need for a "super-effort"—that is, one beyond our ordinary means— was conveyed as an extraordinary ordinary effort, like pushing oneself beyond the point of exhaustion. To an unprepared audience, Gurdjieff could not indicate the practical inner work required either for relating the lower centers or for opening to the higher centers. In later years, with visitors from America and England, he relied on readings from his first book, *Beelzebub's Tales to His Grandson,* as a means of sharing his teaching in allegorical terms.

The esoteric nature of Gurdjieff's teaching was recognized from the beginning by Ouspensky, who was familiar with theosophical writings and had himself traveled to India in search of an esoteric "school." When he met Gurdjieff, he immediately wanted to know what Gurdjieff knew about esotericism and esoteric "schools." As outlined in the biographical notes, he later recognized that his role was to promote the system of ideas—the outer form of the teaching—rather than engage in the inner practice under Gurdjieff. Since both men saw the teaching in terms of esotericism, the separation between them was not the divisive break perceived by their respective followers.

This interpretation, which accepts the exoteric/esoteric distinction in respect of the teaching and the actors, contradicts the established view based on their outer behavior. It is, for me, compelled by two key facts cited in the biographical notes. First, Gurdjieff condemned Ouspensky's independent teaching as a betrayal worthy of Judas Iscariot, when, in fact, Gurdjieff deeply respected Judas as the loyal disciple who alone understood Christ's mission. Then Ouspensky, for his part, selflessly repudiated the System he had taught for twenty-five years, in order to free his followers to migrate to Gurdjieff. These separate, quite extraordinary actions are, in my view, inexplicable unless the two men were all along acting in concert to promote the Fourth Way. To be sure, their secret complicity was never admitted by either of them or by Mme. de Salzmann, who must have known of it. But it was confirmed by her special trip to London in 1947 to invite Ouspensky to Paris to be reunited with Gurdjieff. I was present when, forty years later, she recalled her final meeting with Ouspensky nine months before he died. She said they talked late into the night, with Ouspensky in tears over being unable to come to Paris. It was then that he gave her his manuscript of *Fragments* to take back to Gurdjieff. What touched me most was the way in which she spoke of Ouspensky as an old friend, with a deep affection she could never have felt had he betrayed the man she revered as her master.

STEPHEN A. GRANT

In Search of Being

INTRODUCTION

Go OUT ON A CLEAR STARLIT NIGHT in some open space and look up at the sky, at those millions of worlds over your head. Remember that perhaps on each of them swarm billions of beings, similar or perhaps superior to you in their organization. Look at the Milky Way. The earth cannot even be called a grain of sand in this infinity. It dissolves and vanishes. And with it, you—where are you?

The knowledge of man's relation to the universe has existed from ancient times. The Great Knowledge is always the same, but the form in which it is expressed changes, depending on the place and the epoch. Like language that has evolved over centuries, the form is barely comprehensible to subsequent generations. For the most part it is taken literally and, in this way, the inner content becomes lost.

The Great Knowledge is handed on in succession from age to age, from people to people, from race to race. The great centers of initiation in India, Assyria, Egypt, Greece, illumine the world with a bright light. The revered names of the great initiates, the living bearers of the truth, are handed on reverently from generation to generation. Truth is fixed by means of symbolical writings and legends, and is transmitted to the mass of people for preservation in the form of customs and ceremonies, in oral traditions, in memorials, in sacred art through the invisible quality in dance, music, sculpture and various rituals. It is communicated openly after a definite trial to those who seek it, and is preserved by oral transmission in the chain of those who know. After a certain time has elapsed, the centers of initiation die out one after the other, and the ancient knowledge departs through underground channels into the deep, hiding from the eyes of the seekers. The bearers of this knowledge also hide, becoming unknown to those around them. But they do not cease to exist. From time to time separate streams break through to the surface, showing that somewhere deep down in the interior, even in our day, there flows the powerful ancient stream of true *knowledge of being*.

To break through to this stream, to find it—this is the task and the aim of the search. For, having found it, a person can entrust himself boldly to the way by which he intends to go. Then there only remains "to know" in order "to be" and "to do." The principle of self-knowledge is clear: *In order to know, it is necessary to find out how to know.*

On this way the seeker will not be entirely alone. At difficult moments he will receive support and guidance, for all who follow this way are connected by an uninterrupted chain. The theory of esotericism is that mankind consists of a large outer circle, embracing all human beings, and a small circle of instructed and understanding people at the center. These produce exoteric and esoteric lines of civilization, which are parallel and independent. Invariably one of them overpowers the other and develops while the other fades. A period of esoteric civilization comes when there are favorable external conditions, political and otherwise. Then *knowledge*, clothed in the form of a teaching corresponding to the conditions of time and place, becomes widely spread.

Every religion points to the existence of a common center of knowledge, and in every sacred book this knowledge is expressed, even though people do not wish to know it. In fact, this knowledge is far more accessible than we usually suppose. No one is concealing anything; there is no secret whatsoever. But great labor and effort are necessary to acquire and transmit true knowledge, both of the person who gives and of the one who receives. And those who have this knowledge are doing everything in their power to share it with as many people as possible, always striving to help them approach it in a state prepared to receive the truth. But in the end knowledge cannot be forced upon anyone, and an impartial survey of the average person's life, of what interests him and fills his day, will show immediately that the whole trouble is that people either do not want this knowledge or are incapable of receiving it.

Anyone who wants knowledge must first himself make an initial effort to find and approach the source on his own. This can be accomplished simply by following the signs that, though available to us all, people generally refuse to see or recognize. Knowledge will never come to us by itself. We understand this very well as far as ordinary knowledge is concerned, but with Great Knowledge, when we admit the possibility of its existence, we somehow expect something different. We all know full well that if, for instance, a person wants to master Chinese, this will take several years of hard work. We know that five years are required to grasp the principles of medicine, and perhaps even twice as much for painting or music. And yet there are theories claiming that we can acquire *knowledge* without any effort at all, even *in our sleep*. The very existence of such theories demonstrates yet again why knowledge is still inaccessible to us. At the same time, however, we need to understand that our *independent efforts* to attain anything of this sort cannot possibly succeed. We can only attain knowledge with the help of those who already possess it. *One must learn from those who know.*

Our present knowledge is based on sense perception—like children's. If we wish to acquire knowledge of reality, we must change ourselves, opening to a higher state of consciousness through development of our being. Change of knowledge comes from change of being. We must first have self-knowledge, and with the help of self-knowledge we shall learn how to change ourselves—if we wish to change ourselves. Systems and schools can indicate methods and ways, so that when we are ready new knowledge will come to us from outside. But no system or school whatever can do our work for us—we have to do it ourselves. Inner growth, a change of being, depends entirely upon the work that a person must do himself.

In the chapters that follow, many things will be explained schematically, including the laws of unity that are reflected in all phenomena. But when we use words dealing with objective knowledge, with unity in diversity, attempts at literal understanding lead to delusion. So, do not take anything literally. Try simply to grasp the principle, so that understanding becomes deeper and deeper. In this teaching the first principle is that nothing is to be taken on faith. One should believe nothing that cannot be verified for oneself.

I

KNOW THYSELF

WHAT ARE WE?

WHEN SPEAKING ON DIFFERENT SUBJECTS, we may notice
how difficult it is to pass on our understanding, even of the most
ordinary subject and to a person well known to us. Our language is too
poor for full and exact descriptions. This gap in understanding between
one person and another is a mathematically ordered phenomenon as
precise as the multiplication table. It depends in general on the so-called
"psyche" of the people concerned, and in particular on the state of their
psyche at any given moment.

The truth of this law can be verified at every step. In order to be
understood by another person, it is necessary not only for the speaker
to know how to speak but for the listener to know how to listen. We
must first establish the possibility of a common understanding. For this
we each have to look at things, especially at ourselves, from a point of
view, from an angle, that may be different from what is usual or natural
to us. Only to look—for to do more is possible only with the wish and
cooperation of the listener, only when the listener ceases to be passive
and begins to listen in an active state.

Very often in conversation with people, one hears the direct or im-
plied view that man as we encounter him in ordinary life could be regarded as almost the center of the universe, the "crown of creation," or
at any rate that he is a great and important entity, that his possibilities
and powers are almost unlimited. But even with such views there are

7

a number of reservations. We say that, for this, exceptional conditions are necessary, special circumstances, inspiration, revelation and so on.

If, however, we examine this conception of "man," we see at once that it is made up of features that belong not to one person but to a number of known or supposed separate individuals. We never meet such a person in real life, neither in the present nor as a historical personage of the past. For each and every one of us has his own weaknesses, and if we look closely, the mirage of greatness and power dissolves. Yet the most interesting thing is not that we clothe others in this mirage, but that, owing to a peculiar feature of our own psyche, we each transfer it to ourselves, if not in its entirety, at least in part as a reflection. And so, although all of us are ordinary human beings, we imagine ourselves to be that collective type, or not far removed from it.

If we knew how to be really sincere with ourselves—not as the word is usually understood, but mercilessly honest—then, to the question "What are we?" we would not expect a comforting reply. Yet, as we are, almost all of us would be puzzled and answer with another question: "What do you mean?" And we would then realize that we have lived all our lives without asking ourselves this question, that we have taken for granted, as axiomatic, that we are "something," even something valuable, something we have never doubted. At the same time, we are unable to explain to another person what this something is, unable to convey even any idea of it, for we ourselves do not know what it is. Is the reason we do not know because, in fact, this "something" does not exist, but is merely assumed to exist? Is it not strange that we pay so little attention to ourselves, with no real interest in self-knowledge? Is it not strange how we shut our eyes to what we really are, and spend our lives in the reassuring conviction that we represent something of value? We fail to see the emptiness hidden behind the facade created by our self-delusion, and do not realize that this value is purely conventional.

True, this is not always so. Not everyone looks at himself superficially. There do exist inquiring minds that long for the truth of the heart, seek it, strive to solve the problems set by life, try to penetrate into the essence of things and to understand themselves. If we reason and think soundly, no matter what path we follow in solving these problems, each of us must inevitably arrive back at ourselves. We must begin with the solution of the problem of what we are ourselves and of our place in the world around us. For without this knowledge, we will have no center of gravity in our search. Socrates's words "Know thyself" remain a guiding principle for all who seek true knowledge and *being*.

We have just used a new word—"being"—by which it is important that we all understand the same thing. We have been questioning whether what we think about ourselves corresponds to what we are in reality. One person, for example, is a doctor, another an engineer, or an artist. Are we in reality what we think we are? Can we define ourselves as synonymous with our profession, with the experience that it, or preparation for it, has given us?

Our picture of ourselves is formed by what we experience. Each of us comes into the world unsoiled, like a clean sheet of paper. Then people and circumstances around us begin vying with each other to sully this sheet, to cover it with writing. Education, the formation of morals, information called "knowledge"—all feelings of duty, honor, conscience and so on—enter here. And all these people claim that the methods adopted for grafting these shoots known as man's "personality" to the trunk are immutable and infallible. Gradually the sheet is soiled, and the more covered with so-called "knowledge" it becomes, the cleverer we are considered to be. The more writing in the place called "duty," the more honest we are said to be. So it is with everything. And we, seeing that people regard this soiled veneer as merit, consider it valuable. This is an example of what we call "man," to which we often even add such words as "talent" and "genius." Yet such a genius will have his mood spoiled for the whole day if he does not find his slippers by his bed when he wakes up in the morning.

We do not realize that we are not free either in our manifestations or in our life. None of us can be what we wish to be and what we think we are. None of us is like our picture of ourselves, and the words "man, the crown of creation" do not apply to us. "Man"—this is a proud term. But we must ask ourselves: what kind of man? Not the person, surely, who is irritated at trifles, who gives his attention to petty matters and is distracted by everything around him. To have the right to call oneself "man," we must actually *be* man. And this "being" comes only through self-knowledge and development in directions that become clear through self-knowledge.

Have we ever tried to observe ourselves when our attention has not been concentrating on some definite problem? Most of us are familiar with this, although perhaps only a few have systematically watched it in ourselves. We are no doubt aware of the way we think by chance association, when our thought strings together disconnected scenes and memories, when everything that falls within the field of consciousness, or merely touches it lightly, calls up chance associations. The string of thoughts seems to go on uninterruptedly, weaving together fragments of former perceptions from different recordings in our memory. And these recordings play continuously while the apparatus of our thinking deftly weaves threads of thought from this material. Our feelings go on in the same way, agreeable and disagreeable—joy and sorrow, laughter and irritation, pleasure and pain, sympathy and antipathy. We hear ourselves praised and we are pleased; someone reproves us and our mood is spoiled. Something new captures our interest and instantly makes us forget what interested us as strongly the moment before. Gradually our interest is attached to the new thing, eventually to such an extent that we sink into it from head to foot. Suddenly we are possessed, captivated by it. We have disappeared. And this propensity to be captivated, this infatuation, is a property of each one of us under many different guises. It binds us, taking away our strength and time, and leaving us no possibility to be objective and free—two essential qualities for anyone who would follow the way of self-knowledge.

If we wish for self-knowledge, we must strive for freedom. The aim of self-knowledge and the possibility of self-development are of such importance and seriousness—they demand such intensity of effort—that to attempt this in any old way and among other interests is impossible. If we undertake this aim, we must put it first in our life, which is not so long that we can afford to squander it on trifles. In order to be able to spend our time profitably in our search, we need freedom from every kind of attachment. Freedom and seriousness. Not the kind of seriousness that looks out from under furrowed brows with pursed lips, carefully restrained gestures and words filtered through the teeth, but the kind of seriousness that means determination and persistence, intensity and constancy in the undertaking, so that, even when resting, we continue in the search.

Let us each ask ourselves: are we free? If we are relatively secure in a material sense and do not have to worry about tomorrow, if we depend on no one for our livelihood or in the choice of our conditions of life, we are inclined to answer yes. But the freedom we need is not a question of external circumstances. It is a matter of our inner structure and our attitude toward these inner conditions. But perhaps we think that our incapacity is only true for our automatic associations, that with regard to things we "know" the situation is different.

In the course of our life we are learning all the time, and we call the results of this learning "knowledge." Yet, despite this knowledge, we often prove to be ignorant, remote from real life and therefore ill-adapted to it. Most of us are half-educated, like tadpoles, or more often simply "educated" people with a little information about many things, all of it fuzzy and inadequate. Indeed, it is merely information. We cannot call it knowledge, because knowledge is an inalienable property of a person. It cannot be more, it cannot be less. For a person *knows* only when *he himself is that knowledge.* As for our convictions—have we never known them to change? Do they not also fluctuate like everything else in us? It would be more accurate to call them opinions rather than convictions, dependent as much on our mood as on our information, or perhaps simply on the state of our digestion at a given moment.

Every one of us is a rather ordinary example of an animated automaton. We may think that a "soul," and even a "spirit," is necessary to act and to live as we live. But perhaps it is enough to have a key for winding up the spring of our mechanism. Our daily portions of food help wind us up, and renew the aimless antics of our associations, again and again. From these, separate thoughts are selected. We attempt to connect them into a whole and pass them off as valuable, and as our own. We also pick from feelings and sensations, moods and experiences. And out of all this we create the mirage of an inner life. We call ourselves conscious and reasoning beings, talk about God, eternity, eternal life and other higher matters. We speak about everything imaginable, judge and discuss, define and evaluate. We omit, however, to speak about ourselves and about our own real, objective value. For we are all convinced that we can acquire anything that may be lacking in us.

As already said, there are people who hunger and thirst for truth. If we examine the problems of life and are sincere with ourselves, we become convinced that it is no longer acceptable to live as we have lived and to be what we have been until now. A way out of this situation is essential. Yet we can develop our potential capacities only after cleaning out the material that has clogged our machine over the course of our lives. In order to undertake this in a rational way, we have to see what needs to be cleaned, and where and how. And to see this for oneself is almost impossible. In order to see anything of this, we have to look objectively, from the outside. For this, mutual help is necessary.

This is the state of things in the realm of self-knowledge. In order to "do" we must *know*, but to know we must find out *how to know*. We cannot find this out by ourselves.

MAN CANNOT "DO"

F OR AN EXACT STUDY, an exact language is needed. But the ordinary language in which we speak, set forth what we know and understand, and write books does not suffice for even a small amount of
this. An inexact speech cannot serve an exact knowledge. The words are
too broad, too foggy and indefinite, while the meaning put into them is
too arbitrary and variable. They cannot have any constant meaning. Yet
we have no way to indicate the meaning and the particular nuance we
attach to each word, that is, the relation in which it is taken by us. And
we do not aim at this. On the contrary, we invariably wish to establish
our personal meaning for a word and to take it always in that sense,
which is obviously impossible as one and the same word used at different times and in various ways has different meanings.

The wrong use of words and the qualities of the words themselves
have made them unreliable instruments of an exact speech and knowledge, not to mention that we have neither words nor expressions for
many notions accessible to our reason. The language of numbers alone
can serve for an exact expression, but this language is applied only to
designate and compare quantities. Yet things do not differ only in size,
and their definition from the quantitative point of view is not sufficient
for an exact knowledge and analysis. We do not know how to apply
the language of numbers to attributes, how to designate qualities nu-
merically in relation to some constant. If this could be done, we could
express ourselves in an exact language. Nevertheless, we need to bring

our thinking closer to a precise mathematical designation of things and events, and to find the possibility of understanding ourselves and each other.

If we take any of the most commonly used words and try to see their varied meanings according to who uses them and how, we shall see why we have no power to express our thoughts exactly, and why everything we think and say is so unstable and contradictory. Apart from the variety of meanings for every word, this confusion and contradiction are caused by the fact that we never define for ourselves the precise sense in which we take a particular word, and only wonder why others do not understand something so clear to us. For example, if the word "world" is said in the company of ten people, each one of them will understand the word in his own way. If we knew how to catch and write down our own thoughts, we would see that we have no ideas connected with the word "world," but that merely a well-known expression and a familiar sound have been uttered, the significance of which is supposed to be known. It is as if each of us hearing the word says to ourselves: "Ah, the 'world,' I know what it is." As a matter of fact, we do not really know at all. But the word is familiar and, therefore, no questioning occurs to us—it is just accepted. A question comes only in respect of new words that we do not recognize, and then we tend to substitute a known word for the unknown. We call this "understanding."

If we now ask ourselves what we understand by the word "world," we will be perplexed by such a question. Usually, when we hear or use this word in conversation, we do not think about what it means, having decided once and for all that we know and that everybody knows. Now, for the first time, we see that we do not know and that we have never thought about it. But we will not be able and will not know how to remain with the thought of our ignorance. We are not capable enough of observing nor sufficiently sincere with ourselves. We will soon recover, that is, we will quickly deceive ourselves. And we will remember or hastily compose a definition of the word "world" from some familiar source, or borrow the first definition of someone else that enters our head. Then we will express this as our own understanding, although we have never really thought about the word and, in fact, do not even know what we have thought.

Nevertheless, if the question were approached in the right way, we could establish quite accurately what we understand by this word. And from a right understanding, this definition would include in itself all views about the world and all approaches to the question. Having thus agreed on such a definition, we would be able to speak to one another about the world. Indeed, it is only by starting from such a definition that we can understand each other. This is because, in fact, we live at one and the same time in six worlds, just as we live on a floor of such and such a house, in such and such a street, town, state and continent. If we speak about the place where we live without indicating whether we are referring to the house or the town or the part of the world, we certainly will not be understood. But we always speak in this way about things having no practical importance. By a single word we designate too readily a series of notions that are related in the same way a negligible part is related to an enormous whole.

An exact speech should point out always and quite precisely in what relation each notion is taken and what it includes in itself—that is, of what parts it consists and into what it enters as a component part. Logically this is intelligible and irrefutable, but unfortunately it never comes to pass, if only for the reason that we often do not know, and do not know how to find, the different parts and the relations of the given notion. An important principle of this teaching is to make clear the relativity of every notion, not in the abstract sense that everything in the world is relative but indicating exactly in what and how it relates to the rest.

If we now take the notion "man," we shall again see the misunderstanding of this word, we shall see that the same contradictions are put into it. We all use this word and think we understand what "man" means. But, as a matter of fact, each of us understands it in our own way, and all in different ways. The learned naturalist sees in man a perfected breed of monkey and defines man by the construction of the teeth and so on. The religious person, who believes in God and the future life, sees in man his immortal soul confined in a perishable terrestrial envelope, which is surrounded by temptations and leads him into danger. The economist considers man as a producing and consuming entity. And so on. All these views seem entirely opposed to one another, contradicting one another and having no points of contact. Moreover, the question is further complicated by the fact that we see among men many differences, so great and so sharply defined that it often seems strange to use the single term "man" to refer to all these different beings.

And, if, in the face of all this, we each ask ourselves what man is, we see that we cannot answer the question—we do not know. Neither anatomically, physiologically, psychologically, nor economically do the definitions suffice, as they relate to all aspects equally without allowing us to distinguish differences that we see. Although our store of information is quite sufficient for determining what man is, we do not know how to approach the matter in a simple way. We ourselves complicate and muddle the question.

For this teaching, man is defined as the being who can "do"—that is, act consciously and according to one's will. We cannot find a more complete definition. Animals differ from plants by their power of locomotion. And although a mollusk attached to a rock, and also certain seaweeds capable of moving against the current, seem to violate this principle, the law is nevertheless quite true—a plant can neither hunt for food, avoid a shock, nor hide itself from its pursuer. Man differs from the animal by his capacity for conscious action, his capacity for doing. We cannot deny this, and we see that this definition satisfies all requirements. It makes it possible to single out man from other beings not possessing the power of conscious action, and at the same time to differentiate a person according to the degree of consciousness in his action.

Without exaggeration we can say that all the differences which strike us among people can be reduced to the differences in the consciousness of their actions. They seem to vary so much just because the actions of some are, according to our opinion, deeply conscious, while the actions of others are so unconscious that they even seem to surpass the unconsciousness of stones, which at least react rightly to external phenomena. The question is complicated by the fact that often the same person shows us, side by side with what appear to be entirely conscious acts of will, other, quite unconscious animal-mechanical reactions. By virtue of this, man appears to us to be an extraordinarily complicated being. This teaching denies this complication and puts before us a difficult paradox: Man is he who can "do," but among ordinary people, as well as those who are considered extraordinary, there is no one who can "do."

In personal, family and social life, in politics, science, art, philosophy, and religion, everything from beginning to end is "done." Nobody can "do" anything. If two of us, beginning a conversation about man, agree to call him a being capable of action, of "doing," we will always understand one another. Certainly we will make sufficiently clear what "doing" means, that it requires a high degree of being and of knowledge. Ordinarily we do not even understand what "doing" means, because, in our own case and in everything around us, everything is always "done" and has always been "done."

A person who sleeps cannot "do." With him everything is done in sleep. Sleep is understood here not in the literal sense of organic sleep, but in the sense of a state of associative existence. First of all, we must awake. Having awakened, we will see that as we are, we cannot "do." Then we will have to die voluntarily and be reborn. Once reborn, we must grow and learn. When we have grown and know, then we will be able to "do."

The idea that man cannot "do" and that everything is "done" in him coincides with positivist science. According to this view, man is a complicated organism that has developed through evolution from the simplest organism and is capable of reacting in a complex manner to external impressions. This capacity for reaction is so complicated, and the answering response may be so remote from the cause that called and conditioned it, that a person's actions, or at least a part of them, seem to a naive observer to be voluntary and independent. As a matter of fact, man is not capable of even the smallest independent or spontaneous action. The whole of him is nothing but the result of external influences. Man is a process, a transmitting station of forces. If we imagine a person deprived from his birth of all impressions, with his life preserved by some miracle, such a person would not be capable of a single action or movement. In actual fact he could not live, as he could neither breathe nor eat. Life is a complicated series of actions—breathing, eating, interchange of matter, growth of cells and tissues, reflexes, nervous impulses and so on. In a person lacking external impressions none of this would be possible. And, of course, he could not accomplish actions that are usually regarded as voluntary and conscious.

Thus, from the positivist point of view, man differs from animals only by the greater complexity of his reactions to external impressions, and by a longer interval between the impression and the reaction. But man, like animals, is incapable of independent action of his own, and what we call "will" in man is nothing but the resultant of his desires. Such is a clearly positivist view. But there are very few who sincerely and consistently hold it. Most of us, while assuring ourselves and others that we stand on the ground of a strictly scientific positivist world-concept, actually hold a mixture of theories. We recognize the positivist view of things only up to a certain point, that is, until it begins to be too austere and offers too little consolation. On the one hand, we recognize that all physical and psychical processes in man are only reflexes, but at the same time we assume a certain independent consciousness, a certain spiritual principle—free will.

Will, from this teaching's viewpoint, is a specific combination derived from qualities that are specially developed and exist in a person capable of "doing." It is a sign of a very high level of being as compared with the being of an ordinary person. Only those who have such being can "do." All the rest of us are merely automatons, put into action by external forces. We are like a simple machine or mechanical toy, which functions only as long as the spring within it unwinds, and is not capable of adding anything to its force. There are great possibilities in man, far greater than recognized by positivist science, but as we are now, we have no claim to being an entity with independence and will.

NO UNIFIED "I"

W E ORDINARILY LIVE exercising only a minute part of our functions and strength. This is because we do not know ourselves. We do not recognize that we are machines, and do not know the nature and working of our mechanism. We are *machines*.

Man is born, it is said, with a mechanism created for receiving many kinds of impressions. The perception of some of these impressions begins before birth, and during his growth more and more receiving apparatuses appear and become perfected. The structure of these apparatuses is the same in all the parts of the machine, analogous to blank discs on which music is recorded. On these "discs" all the impressions are engraved, from the first day of life and even before. In addition, a mechanism automatically allows all new impressions to be connected with those previously recorded, and a chronological record is kept. Thus every impression that has been experienced is recorded in several places on several discs, where it is preserved intact. What we call memory is a very imperfect device by which we make use of only a small part of our store of impressions. But once experienced, impressions never disappear; they are preserved on the discs where they are recorded. Many experiments in hypnosis have proved that a person remembers everything he has ever experienced, down to the minutest detail. All the particularities of our worldview, and the characteristic features of our individuality, depend on the order in which these recordings were made and upon the quality of the engraved discs existing in us.

The operation of our associative mechanism determines how we think and feel. Suppose that some impression has been experienced and recorded in connection with another impression having nothing in common with the first—for instance, a bright dance tune has been heard in a moment of intense psychic shock, distress or sorrow. Then this bright tune will always evoke in us the same negative emotion, and, correspondingly, the feeling of distress will recall that tune. Our science calls this associative thinking and feeling. But science does not realize how much man is bound by these associations and how he cannot get away from them. Our thinking and feeling are entirely determined by the character and quality of these associations.

One of our greatest errors is our illusion in regard to our "I." Man such as we know him—the "human machine" who cannot "do" and all of whose seeming actions simply are "done"—cannot have an invariable and unified "I." Our "I" changes as frequently as our thoughts, feelings and moods, and we make a serious mistake in considering ourselves always the same person, when actually we are *always someone else* and never the same person as a moment ago. *Man has no constant and invariable "I."* Every thought, every mood, every desire, every sensation says "I." And, in each case, we assume that this "I" speaks for the *Whole*, the whole person, and that a thought, desire or aversion represents the expression of this Whole. In actual fact this assumption is entirely baseless. Each thought and desire appears and lives quite separately and independently of the Whole. And the Whole never actually expresses itself, for the simple reason that it exists, as such, only as a material entity in a physical body and as an abstract concept. In his psyche, man has no unified "I," but rather hundreds of separate small "I's" that are very often either entirely unknown and inaccessible to one another or, on the contrary, hostile to one another, that is, mutually exclusive and incompatible. Each minute, each moment, we are saying or thinking "I," and each time, our "I" is different. First it is a thought, then a desire, then a sensation, then another thought and so on, ad infinitum. *Man is a plurality;* his name is Legion.

The alternation of "I's," their constant struggle for supremacy, is directed by accidental external influences. Warmth, sunshine, nice weather—all these things immediately call up an entire group of "I's." Cold, fog, rain, call up another group, with different associations, feelings and actions. There is nothing in us capable of controlling the change of "I's." This is largely due to the fact that we are not aware of the change, but live always in the last "I." Naturally, some "I's" are stronger than others. This is not due to their own conscious strength, but is merely the result of accidents or mechanical external stimuli. Factors like upbringing, role models, reading, the hypnotism of religion, or caste and tradition, can create "I's" in our personality that are strong enough to dominate whole sets of other, weaker "I's." But their strength is determined by the recording discs in our receiving apparatuses. And all the "I's" making up our personality have the same origin as these discs. Both the stronger and weaker "I's" are the results of external stimuli, and are set in motion and controlled by fresh influences from outside.

Let us reiterate: Man has no individuality, no single, unified "I," but is divided into a multiplicity of small "I's." Each of these separate small "I's" is able to call itself by the name of the Whole, to act in the name of the Whole, to agree or disagree, give promises, make decisions, with which another "I" or the Whole will have to deal. This explains why people so often make decisions and so seldom carry them out. For example, a person decides that, starting tomorrow, he will get up early each day. This is decided by one "I," or perhaps a group of "I's," but it turns out that the "I" responsible for getting out of bed completely disagrees with the earlier decision, or perhaps does not even know about it. Naturally, this person will again go on sleeping in the morning, and in the evening he will again decide to get up early the next day. In some cases this phenomenon can have very unpleasant consequences. One small accidental "I" may spontaneously promise something, not to itself but to someone else, at a certain moment on a whim or simply out of vanity. Then it disappears, but the person, that is—the whole combination of other "I's" who are completely innocent of the action of this "I"—may end up paying for it all his life. It is the tragedy of the human condition that every small "I" has the right to sign checks and make binding promises, and the person, that is, the Whole, has to meet them. People's entire lives often consist in paying off or discharging the promises of small, accidental "I's."

Our chief delusion is our conviction that we can "do," that we have power to act, to do things. But actually humanity in its current state is incapable of doing anything. Everything that humanity is occupied with simply is "done." *Everything* that occurs around us, *everything* that is accomplished by us, *everything* that comes from us—*everything happens*. And it happens just as rain results from changes in temperature of various layers of the atmosphere, as snow melts under the rays of the sun, and as water freezes at a certain temperature. Man is a machine. Everything we do, all our actions, words, thoughts, feelings, convictions, opinions and habits are brought about by external influences and impressions. We cannot produce a single thought or action on our own. Everything we say, do, think, feel—all this just happens. We cannot discover anything, invent anything. It all is "done," it all happens on its own.

To internalize this fact for oneself, to understand it, to be convinced of its truth, one must get rid of a thousand illusions about man, about our ability to create or control our own lives. Everything that we think we do just happens—popular movements, wars, revolutions, changes in government, all this simply happens. The same is true of everything that occurs in the life of an individual person. We are born, live, die, build houses, write books, not as we want to, but simply because that is how things work out. We cannot do, build, destroy, write or imagine, but *are merely a part of the doing, building, destruction, writing and imagination that occur.* We cannot love, hate or desire, but merely *experience love, hate and desire.* Everything has a necessary cause in something else.

People believe in progress and culture, but *there is no such thing as progress.* Everything is just as it was thousands, or even tens of thousands, of years ago. Appearances may change, but the essence of things does not. Humanity is always the same. The lives of "civilized" and "cultured" people revolve around exactly the same interests as the most ignorant savages. Modern civilization is based on violence and slavery, and fine words.

Yet "progress" and "civilization," in the real sense of these terms, cannot happen by themselves, as the result of unconscious, mechanical actions. They can come about only as the result of *conscious* efforts. But what kind of conscious effort can machines be capable of? And if one machine acts unconsciously, then a hundred machines also act unconsciously, and the same is true for a thousand, or a hundred thousand or a million machines. The unconscious activity of a *million machines* must necessarily result in destruction and extermination. It is precisely these unconscious, involuntary actions that are the root of all evil.

One particular aspect is the question about war. People ask how to stop wars, but wars cannot be stopped, because they result from the slavery in which we live. Strictly speaking, man is not to blame for war, which in fact is due to planetary influences on a cosmic scale. But we put up no resistance whatever to these influences, and we cannot resist them, because we are slaves. If we were free and were capable of "doing," we would be able to resist these influences and refrain from killing one another. We are what we are and cannot be different. War has many causes that are unknown, some in us, others outside us. We must begin with the causes that reside in ourselves, recognizing that there is no possibility to be independent of cosmic forces when we are the slave of everything that surrounds us. We have to see that we are controlled by everything around us. If we can achieve freedom from surrounding things, we may then become free from planetary influences.

Freedom, liberation—this must be our aim. To become free, to escape from slavery—it is for this that we must strive if we have any understanding at all of our current position. So long as we remain slaves both inwardly and outwardly, we can accomplish nothing and we can never escape the slavery of circumstance. But we cannot cease to be a slave to external conditions while we remain enslaved inwardly. In order to become free, we must achieve inner freedom. The primary reason for our inner slavery is our ignorance, that is, our ignorance of ourselves. Without self-knowledge, we cannot be free, we cannot govern ourselves. Without understanding the way our machine works, we will always remain a slave, the plaything of the forces that act upon us.

It is necessary first of all *to know the machine*. Of course, a machine, a real machine, does not and cannot know itself. In fact, when a machine knows itself, it is no longer merely a machine, or, at least, not such as it was before. It already begins to be *responsible* for its actions. To know our machine, we must realize our own situation. We are in prison. All we can wish for, if we are sensible, is to escape. But how? The only way out is to tunnel under a wall. This is too great a task for one person alone. But if there are ten or twenty people, working in shifts, some digging, some covering for others, then they may be able to tunnel out and escape. Furthermore, no one can escape from prison without the help of those *who have already escaped*. Only they can tell how to get out, or provide whatever tools might be needed. But there is no way *one* prisoner acting alone could find these people or communicate with them. What is needed is an organized group. Nothing can be achieved without an organized group.

If a person in prison wants to have any chance at escape, the first thing he must do is *realize that he is in prison*. So long as we fail to recognize this, we have no chance whatever. No one can set us free by force; no one can help us escape if we do not want to leave. Liberation, if it can be attained, will come only as a result of work and efforts—above all, of conscious efforts, toward a definite aim.

TOWARD SELF-KNOWLEDGE

T HE CALL TO "KNOW THYSELF" is generally ascribed to Socrates, but these words actually serve as the basis for many systems and schools of even greater antiquity. Modern thought is aware of this principle, albeit with a vague understanding of its meaning and significance. The typical educated person today, even one with philosophic or scientific interests, does not realize that the principle "Know thyself" refers to the need to know one's machine, the "human machine" that is more or less the same in all people. It is a call, in the first place, to study the structure, functions and laws of our organism. All the parts of the human machine are so interconnected, with each thing dependent upon another, that it is completely impossible to study any single function without studying all the others. So, at least in regard to the human machine, we must know *everything* in order to know anything in us. And this actually is possible. But it requires time and effort, and, above all, the application of the right method under the proper guidance.

The principle "Know thyself" is a rich and profound imperative. It demands, first of all, that a person who wants to know himself understand what it means, what it entails, and what it requires. In fact, to know oneself is a huge, but very vague and distant, aim—way beyond our present capacity. Therefore, strictly speaking, we cannot even claim it as our actual goal. Rather than striving for self-knowledge, we have to content ourselves for the time being with self-study, accepting this as our immediate objective. The aim must therefore be to begin to study oneself, to *know oneself*, in the right way. Self-study is the work, the way, that will ultimately lead to self-knowledge. But before we can undertake self-study, we must first learn *how to study*, where to begin, what methods to use.

The primary method of self-study is self-observation, which is necessary in order to understand how the various functions of the human machine are related to one another. This in turn will allow us to understand how and why on specific occasions everything is "done" in us. This basic grasp of the functions and characteristics of the human machine is a prerequisite for understanding the fundamental principles of its activity. Without knowing these principles and constantly bearing them in mind, any attempt at self-observation will be inherently flawed. Thus, for real self-knowledge, the kind of introspection in which people ordinarily engage over the course of their lives is of no use and leads nowhere.

We have to understand that each of our normal psychic functions is a means of acquiring a certain kind of knowledge. The mind allows us to perceive one aspect of things and events, emotions another aspect and sensations a third. We can, however, have the fullest knowledge of something only if we examine it simultaneously with our mind, feeling and sensation. This level of perception, which is possible only with a different level of being, should be the goal of every person who strives for true knowledge.

In ordinary conditions we see the world through a glass darkly, but even if we recognize this, we are still powerless to change it. Our mode of perception depends on the functioning of our organism as a whole. All of our functions are interconnected, interdependent, and they all seek to maintain a state of mutual equilibrium. Therefore, as we begin to study ourselves, we must understand that if we discover an aspect that we dislike, we will not be able to change it. To study is one thing, to change is something else altogether. But study is the first step toward realizing the potential for change in the future. In the beginning, we must understand that for a long time all our work will be dedicated to study alone.

II

OUR HUMAN MACHINE

FUNCTIONS AND CENTERS

T HE IDEA OF MAN as a machine must be clearly understood, and it must be represented to oneself in order to see its significance and all its implications. This teaching gives general principles of the structure of the mechanism. But this is only as a plan for one's own self-observation. The first principle is that nothing be taken on faith.

Our main error lies in assuming that we have *a single mind*, whose functions are "conscious," and that everything that does not enter this mind is "unconscious" or "subconscious." The activity of the human machine is controlled not by one mind but by several *minds*, which are entirely independent of each other, with distinct functions and separate spheres of activity. This must be understood first of all, because unless this is recognized, nothing can be understood about our functioning.

The human machine has five ordinary functions:

Thinking
Feeling
Moving
Instinctive
Sex

For us, self-study must begin with the first four functions: thinking, feeling, moving and instinctive. Sex function is conditioned by these four and can be studied only later when the others have been sufficiently understood.

For most of us it is clear what we mean by the thinking or intellectual function: mental processes like forming representations and concepts, reasoning, comparison, affirmation, negation, forming words,
imagination. The second function is feeling or emotions, including joy,
sorrow, fear, astonishment and so on. We think it is clear how emotions
differ from thoughts, but we often mix them in our ordinary thinking
and speaking.

The two other functions, moving and instinctive, take longer to understand, because they are not rightly divided in ordinary psychology.
The words "instinct" and "instinctive" generally are used in the wrong
sense, particularly as applied to external functions that are in reality
moving functions, and sometimes emotional. The moving function
governs all external movements, such as walking, writing, speaking and
eating. This includes external movements that in ordinary language are
called "instinctive," such as catching a falling object without thinking.
The moving function is also responsible for useless inner movements
like imagining, daydreaming, talking to oneself, talking for talking's
sake, and, generally, all uncontrolled manifestations.

The instinctive function includes all the inner work of the organism, such as digestion, breathing, and blood circulation; the five senses;
all physical feeling, that is, sensations which are either pleasant or unpleasant; and all reflexes, including laughter and yawning.

The difference between the moving and instinctive functions is
clear and can be easily understood. None of the moving functions is
inherent and one has to learn them all, as a child learns to walk or to
write. On the other hand, all instinctive functions without exception are
inherent and do not have to be learned.

According to accepted psychology, our thinking functions are
controlled by a certain *center* that we call "mind" or "intellect," or the
"brain." And this is quite right. At the same time, however, we must
understand that each of the other functions is also controlled by its own
center or mind. Thus, from the point of view of this teaching, there are
four minds that control our ordinary actions: thinking, feeling, moving and instinctive mind, which we shall call "centers." Each center is

independent of the others, having its own sphere of action, powers, and ways of development.

In reality *each center occupies the whole body,* penetrates, so to speak, the whole organism. At the same time, each has what is called its "center of gravity." The center of gravity of the thinking center is in the brain. The center of gravity of the feeling center is in the solar plexus. And the centers of gravity of the moving and instinctive centers are in the spinal cord. All four centers have much in common and, at the same time, each has its own peculiar characteristics.

One of the most important characteristics of centers is the great difference in the speed of their functioning. *The slowest is the thinking center.* Next—although very much faster—are the moving and instinctive centers, which have more or less the same speed. The fastest of all is the feeling center, though in our ordinary state it rarely operates at its real speed, and generally works at the speed of the moving and instinctive centers.

Observation can show us the huge difference in the speeds of the functions. We can compare the speed of mental processes with moving functions if we observe ourselves when we perform quick simultaneous movements, as when driving a car or doing physical work requiring quick judgment and action. We see at once that we cannot observe all our movements. We either have to slow them down or miss the greater part of what we are trying to observe. Otherwise, we will risk an accident, and probably make a mistake if we persist in observing. There are many similar observations that can be made, particularly of the feeling center, which is even faster.

Another supposition of this teaching is that each center is divided into positive and negative parts. This division is quite clear in the thinking, moving and instinctive centers. All the work of the thinking center is divided into *affirmation* and *negation,* into *yes* and *no.* At every instant in our thinking, either one part outweighs the other or they come to a moment of equal strength in indecision. The negative part is as useful as the positive, and any diminishing of strength of one in relation to the other results in mental disorder.

In the moving center the division into positive and negative is simply movement as opposed to rest. In the work of the instinctive center the division into positive and negative, or pleasant and unpleasant, is also clear, and both parts are equally necessary for orientation in life.

In the feeling center, at first glance, the division seems obvious and simple if we take pleasant emotions such as joy, affection, self-confidence, as belonging to the positive part, and unpleasant emotions like fear, irritation, envy, as belonging to the negative part. But in reality the issue is more complicated. The feeling center has no positive and no negative part, and in our ordinary state of consciousness we do not have positive emotions or real negative emotions. *Positive emotions are emotions that cannot become negative*—that is, they are understood to be invariable emotions such as "love," "hope," and "faith." But all our pleasant emotions can turn into unpleasant emotions at any moment. Love can turn into jealousy or fear of losing what one loves, or into anger and hatred; hope can turn into daydreaming or expecting impossible things; and faith can turn into superstition and a weak acceptance of comforting nonsense. On the other hand, most of our negative emotions do not belong to the feeling center itself. They are artificial, based on unrelated instinctive emotions that are transformed by imagination and identification. In fact, many of us have never experienced any *real* feeling, so completely is our time occupied with imaginary emotions. To be sure, we experience many kinds of mental suffering that belong to the feeling center—sorrow, grief, fear, apprehension and so on, that are closely related to our lives, like illness, pain and death. But these are very different from negative emotions that are based on imagination and identification.

Besides being divided into positive and negative, each of the centers is divided into three parts that correspond to the centers themselves—that is, "mechanical," "feeling," and "thinking." This can be seen most clearly in the thinking center. A mechanical part works almost automatically and does not require any attention. In the thinking center, this part includes registering impressions, memories and associations. Although unable to "think," unfortunately this mechanical part is always ready to decide questions in a narrow and limited way, reacting always in terms of forms. It is called the "formatory apparatus." The great majority of mankind live all their lives with only the formatory apparatus, rarely touching other parts of the thinking center. The feeling part of the thinking center requires full attention, but this does not require any effort. The attention is attracted and held by the subject itself, often through identification, which usually is called "interest" or "enthusiasm." The thinking part of the center, which includes creation, innovation and discovery, also requires attention, but this must be controlled and maintained by will and effort.

In addition to these four centers, and the sex center, which is also independent but practically never works independently, there are two other centers—the "higher feeling" center for the higher feeling function in the state of *self-consciousness*, and the "higher thinking" center for the higher mental function in the state of *objective consciousness*. These centers are in us, fully developed and working all the time, but their functioning fails to reach our ordinary consciousness. The cause of this lies in the special properties of our so-called "clear consciousness."

STATES OF CONSCIOUSNESS

NEITHER THE PSYCHIC nor the physical functions of man can be understood unless we recognize that they can both work in different states of consciousness. So, we must try to define in general what consciousness is. We can know consciousness only in ourselves. Note that I said *"can* know"; after all, we can only experience consciousness if we actually have it. And we can know that we do not have it, although not at that very moment but later on, when it returns. When consciousness reappears, we can realize that it has been gone for a long time, and we can pinpoint exactly when it left and when it came back. We can also recognize the moments when we are nearer to or further away from consciousness. And by observing its appearance and disappearance in ourselves, we will inevitably see something that we are currently unaware of—that moments of consciousness are extremely short and separated by long intervals of completely unconscious, mechanical activity. We will then see that we can think, feel, act, speak, work, *without being conscious of it.* And once we see in ourselves the brief flashes of consciousness and the extended periods of mechanicalness, we will be able to recognize when others are conscious of what they are doing and when they are not.

Our biggest mistake is in assuming that *we always have consciousness* and, in general, that consciousness is either *always present* or *never present.* In reality, consciousness is continually changing—now we have it, now we don't. Moreover, there are also different degrees or levels of consciousness. Both consciousness and the various degrees must be experienced in ourselves by sensation, by taste. Not only are verbal definitions of no help in this regard but no definitions are possible so long as we do not understand *what* we have to define, so long as we do not distinguish *consciousness* from *potential consciousness*. Since all we have is potential consciousness with the occasional flash of actual consciousness, we cannot define consciousness as such. We can only say that it is a particular kind of "awareness," independent from the mind's activity—first of all, *awareness of oneself,* awareness of *who one is, where one is,* and further, awareness of what one knows, of what one does not know and so on.

Human beings are capable of four different states of consciousness. But ordinary man (what we later call man number one, number two and number three) lives only in the two lowest states and does not have access to the two higher states. Although he may experience brief flashes of higher consciousness, he is unable to understand them, because his thinking about consciousness is too deeply rooted in the ordinary states with which he is familiar.

The two ordinary states of consciousness are *sleep,* the passive state in which we spend anywhere between a third and half of our lives, and the more active state in which we spend the balance of our lives, in which we walk, write and talk, which we call "clear consciousness" or "waking state of consciousness." To call this last state "clear" or "awake" is a joke to anyone who understands what *clear consciousness* ought in reality to be and compares it with the state in which we actually live.

The third state of consciousness is one of self-remembering or, in other words, "self-consciousness," consciousness of one's being. Most of us assume that we have this state or that, at the very least, we can have it if we want it. Indeed, our science and philosophy have overlooked the fact that *we do not possess* this state of consciousness and cannot create it in ourselves simply by deciding that we want it.

The fourth state of consciousness is called "objective consciousness," a state in which a person is able to perceive things *as they are.* All the great religions hint at the possibility of attaining this state, which

they call "enlightenment" or some other ineffable name but which cannot be described in words. Although it is possible to have occasional
flashes of this objective consciousness, the only right way to this state
is by developing the consciousness of self. If this state is artificially induced temporarily in an ordinary person, he will remember nothing
when he returns to his usual state and probably assume only that for
a time he had blacked out. On the other hand, in the state of self-consciousness, it is possible for a person to experience a flash of objective
consciousness and still retain a memory of it afterward.

The capacity to experience the fourth state of consciousness signi-
fies that a person has reached an entirely different state of being, one
that can come about only through profound inner growth from long
and intensive work on oneself. But the third state of consciousness is
something that a person *as he is* ought to possess. The only reason we
do not possess it is that we are living in a wrong way. The truth is that,
as we are, we can experience this state only as a very occasional flash
of insight. That being said, there is a special kind of training that can
allow us to make this state more or less permanent. For most of us,
as educated and thinking people, the chief obstacle to acquiring consciousness of self is that we think we already possess it and everything
connected with it—individuality in the sense of an invariable "I," a will,
the ability to "do," and so on. Of course, a person who thinks he already
has something will not be interested in acquiring it by long and difficult
work.

In order to understand the difference between states of consciousness, let us return to the first state, that is, sleep. This is an entirely
subjective state of consciousness, in which we are immersed in dreams,
whether we remember them or not. Even if real-world impressions
reach us, such as sounds, temperature, the sensation of our own body,
they are transformed into subjective, usually fantastic, dream-images.
Then we wake up. At first, being awake seems to be a quite different
state of consciousness. We can move, talk with other people, make
plans, see and avoid danger and so on. We are, therefore, obviously
much better off awake than asleep. But if we delve more deeply into

this, if we examine our inner world, our thoughts, the causes of our actions, then we will come to realize that things are actually no different from when we were asleep. In fact, things are even worse because, whereas in sleep we are passive and cannot manifest anything, in the waking state we manifest all the time, and the results of all our actions inevitably have consequences for ourselves and those around us. *And yet we do not remember ourselves.* We are a machine that cannot "do" anything; everything with us is "done." We cannot control our thoughts, our imagination, our emotions or the focus of our attention. We live in a subjective world of "I love it," "I hate it," "I like it," "I don't like it," "I want it," "I don't want it," that is, a world of what we think are our likes and dislikes, desires and aversions. We do not see the real world, which is obscured by the veil of our imagination. *We live in sleep.*

What is called "clear consciousness" is sleep, and of a far more dangerous kind than our sleep at night in bed. We can see the effects if we take some event in the life of humanity—for instance, war. Wars are going on at every moment, that is, millions of sleeping people are trying to annihilate millions of other sleeping people. Of course, they would not do this if they were to awake. Everything people do is a result of the fact that they are asleep. We often wonder whether wars can be stopped. Certainly they can if people would only wake up. This seems a small thing but is the hardest of all because this sleep is induced and maintained by the whole world around us.

Both sleep and the waking state of consciousness are equally subjective. Only by beginning to *remember oneself* will a person really awaken. And then everything around us will suddenly take on an entirely different aspect and meaning. We will see that "life" as we know it is *the life of sleeping people,* a life in sleep. Everything people say, everything they do, is all said and done in sleep. It is possible to think for a thousand years, to write entire libraries' worth of books, to postulate millions of theories, but all of this is just a dream, from which it is impossible to awaken. On the contrary, the only thing these dreamed-up books and theories can ever accomplish is to put other people to sleep.

So, how can we wake up? How can we escape from this sleep? These are the most important, the most vital questions that we as human beings can ever confront. But in order to ask these questions, it is necessary to be convinced of the very fact of sleep, which is possible only by trying to wake up. When we realize that we do not remember ourselves and that we can only come to remember ourselves by beginning to wake up, and when at the same time we see by experience how difficult it is to remember oneself, we will then truly understand that we cannot wake up just by wanting to. More precisely, we might say that it is not even possible to wake up on our own, *by oneself*. But if, say, twenty people were to agree that whoever awakens first will wake up the others, they might have a chance after all.

This concept of human life as sleep is nothing new. In fact, from the dawn of time people have been told that they are asleep and that they must wake up. How many times is this said in the Gospels, for instance? "Awake," "Watch," "Sleep not." Christ's disciples slept even when he was saying his final prayer in the Garden of Gethsemane. It is all there, but do we understand it? Most people think that this is just an expression, a metaphor, and completely overlook its true significance. And again it is easy to understand why. In order to understand this, it is necessary to begin to wake up, or at least to try to wake up. So long as we are deeply asleep and wholly immersed in dreams, we cannot even think about the fact that we are asleep. Indeed, if we were ever to realize that we are asleep, we would wake up.

ESSENCE AND PERSONALITY

E VERY HUMAN BEING consists of two parts: *essence* and *personality.*
A person's essence is what is *his own.* His personality is what is
"not his own," that is, what "does not really belong to him" because
he has acquired it from outside. This includes all knowledge acquired
from learning or reflection, all traces of exterior impressions in the
memory, words and movements that have been learned, feelings created by imitation. All this, which does not really belong to him, is "not
his own." All this is personality. Of course, this division into essence
and personality is not recognized in ordinary psychology.

A small child is what he really is, with no personality. He is essence,
and his desires, tastes, his likes and dislikes, reflect his being such as it is.
It is only when so-called "education" begins that personality begins to
develop, formed partly by the intentional influences of other people and
partly by the child's involuntary imitation of them. In this formation, a
great part is also played by the child's "resistance" to those around him
and attempts to hide from them something that is "his own" or "real."

Essence represents the true nature, the truth in man, whereas personality is false. But in proportion as personality develops, essence gradually manifests itself more rarely and feebly. It is very common for a
person's essence to stop growing at an early age and develop no further.
As a result one will often find a grown-up person, even someone intellectual and, in its accepted meaning, highly "educated," who has the essence of a five- or six-year-old child. This means that everything we see

39

in this person is in reality "not his own." What is his true self, that is, his essence, is usually manifested only in his basic instincts and emotions. Although there are some people whose essence has grown in tandem with personality, these represent rare exceptions, especially in the circumstances of urban, cultured life. Essence has a much better chance to develop in those who live closer to nature in conditions of constant struggle and danger. But, as a rule, the personality of such people is undeveloped. They have more of what is their own, but little of what is "not their own." They have no education, and thus no higher culture. Higher culture creates personality and, at the same time, is produced by personality. In effect, the whole of human life—all we call "civilization," all we call "science," "philosophy," "art," and "politics"—is created by people's personality, that is, by what does not truly belong to them, by what in them is "not their own."

When it is fully grown and developed, essence unites everything that is serious and real in us. In fact, we could say that our real "I," our individuality, can grow only from essence, that it is our essence, grown-up, mature. But this depends on work on oneself, on weakening the pressure of personality that impedes the growth of essence. In the average educated person, the personality is active and the essence is passive. So long as this order of things persists, inner growth in us cannot begin. Personality must become passive, and essence must become active.

One might think that less cultured people should have a greater possibility of growth because essence in them is often more highly developed. But, in fact, it is not so, because their personality is insufficiently formed. Work on oneself and inner growth require a certain development of personality, which consists, in large measure, of recorded material resulting from work of the centers. If a person has an insufficiently developed personality, this means he has a lack of recordings, that is, a lack of knowledge and information, a lack of the material upon which work on oneself must be based. Without some store of knowledge, without a certain amount of material "not his own," a person cannot begin to work on himself. He cannot begin to study himself and struggle with his mechanical habits, simply because he will not understand why he should do so. This does not mean that all the ways are closed to him, but the methods and means that are accessible to a person of developed intellect are not available to him.

Evolution is thus equally difficult for a cultured and an uncultured person. A cultured person lives far from nature, in artificial conditions of life, developing his personality at the expense of his essence. A less cultured person, living in more natural conditions, develops his essence at the expense of his personality. In order to begin work on oneself and have the best chance for success, one must be fortunate enough to have a personality and essence that are equally developed.

IMMATERIAL BODIES

A CCORDING TO AN ANCIENT DOCTRINE, whose traces appear in many teachings of various periods, a person who has attained the highest potential human development *consists of four bodies,* composed of substances that gradually become finer, interpenetrate and form four separate organisms, standing in a definite relationship to one another but capable of independent action. The reason four bodies can exist is that the human organism (that is, the physical body) has such a complex organization that, under the right conditions, a new and independent organism can grow inside it, affording a much more convenient and obedient instrument for consciousness than the physical body. The consciousness in this new body is able to exercise complete control over the physical body. Within this second body, under certain conditions, a third body can grow, again having characteristics of its own. The consciousness in this third body has full power and control over the first two bodies, and is also capable of acquiring knowledge that is inaccessible to either of them. Within the third body, under certain conditions, a fourth can grow, with a consciousness that has complete control over the first three bodies and itself.

Each teaching has its own way of defining the four bodies. In Christian terminology, the first body is called the "carnal" body; the second, the "natural" body; the third, the "spiritual" body; and the fourth (in the terminology of *esoteric Christianity*), the "divine" body. In theosophical terminology, the first is the "physical" body, the second the "astral," the third the "mental," and the fourth the "causal" body. In the terminology of certain Eastern teachings, the first body is the "carriage" (body), the second is the "horse" (feelings, desires), the third the "driver" (mind) and the fourth the driver's "master," who is also the owner of the carriage ("I," consciousness, will). These definitions can be pictured as in the following table.

1ST BODY	2ND BODY	3RD BODY	4TH BODY
Carnal body	Natural body	Spiritual body	Divine body
"Carriage" (body)	"Horse" (feelings, desires)	"Driver" (mind)	"Master" ("I," consciousness, will)
Physical body	Astral body	Mental body	Causal body

Some kind of similar divisions may be found in most schools of thought that acknowledge in man something more than the physical body. But almost all these teachings, while repeating in a recognizable form the divisions of the ancient doctrine, have nevertheless forgotten the most important thing of all, namely, that although the more refined bodies can be artificially cultivated under favorable internal and external conditions, no one possesses them from birth. The "astral body" is not something indispensable, but a great luxury that only a few of us can afford. In fact, our physical body is fully capable of performing all the functions necessary for life, and we can live perfectly well without an "astral body." A person with no "astral body" may even come off as a *spiritual person,* that is, one whose life includes a host of intellectual, religious and moral preoccupations, and may fool not only others but himself. This applies still more, of course, to the "mental body" and the fourth body.

Ordinary man does not have these bodies or corresponding functions. But he and others around him often think that he does, for two reasons. First, the physical body works with the same substances that make up the higher bodies, although they do not belong to it and do not crystallize in it. Secondly, the physical body is capable of functions that are analogous to those of the higher bodies, even though they are significantly different. The main difference between the functioning is in the control. In the case of a person who has only a physical body, all the functions are controlled and governed by the body which, in its turn, is governed by external influences. In the case of a person who has a higher body, everything, including the physical body, is controlled by the higher body. The parallel functions of a person of physical body and one of higher bodies may be represented as follows:

Automaton working by external influences	Desires produced by automaton	Thoughts proceeding from desires	Different and contradictory "wills" created by desires

Body obeying desires and emotions which are subject to intelligence	Emotional powers and desires obeying thought and intelligence	Thinking functions obeying consciousness and will	"I" Ego Consciousness Will

In the first case, the physical body, which functions automatically, is dependent upon external influences, while the next three functions are dependent entirely on the body and these external influences. Desires or aversions—"I want," "I don't want," "I like," "I don't like"—are the province of the second body but depend upon chance occurrences that are purely accidental. "Thinking," although corresponding to the functions of the third body, is an entirely mechanical process. And "will," an attribute of the fourth body, is completely absent. Ordinary mechanical man has only incidental desires, whose relative consistency is what most people consider a strong or a weak will.

In the second case, that is, in relation to the functions of the four bodies, the physical body still functions automatically but depends upon the influences of the other bodies. Instead of a mass of different and often contradictory desires, there is *one single "I,"* whole, indivisible and invariable. There is *individuality,* capable of dominating the desires and overcoming both the reluctance and resistance of the physical body. Instead of the mechanical process of thinking, there is *consciousness.* And there is *will,* consisting not merely of contradictory desires of different "I's," but a force issuing from consciousness and governed by individuality, by a single and invariable "I." Only such a will, independent of accident and external influences, can be called "free," for it cannot be altered or directed by outside forces.

An Eastern teaching describes the functions and growth of the four bodies by analogy to a vessel or retort filled with various metal powders. The powders are not interconnected but simply mixed together, so that any accidental change in the position of the retort rearranges their relative distribution. If the retort is shaken or tapped on the outside, the powder on top may end up at the bottom or in the middle, while the one originally at the bottom may end up on top. The distribution of the powders is not at all constant, nor, under such conditions, can it be. The same is true of our emotional and spiritual life. Just as, at any given moment, some new influence may come along and alter the distribution of the powders so that the one on top switches places with the one at the bottom, so it is with us. Science calls this a state of mechanical mixture, in which the essential characteristic is the instability and variability of the interrelation of the powders.

Although it is impossible to stabilize their interrelation in a state of mechanical mixture, the nature of the powders is such that they may be fused. This can be accomplished by lighting a special kind of fire under the retort, which, by heating and melting the powders, eventually causes them to blend and fuse together. Once fused in this way, the powders will be in the state of a chemical compound, an alloy, in which, unlike a mechanical mixture, they can no longer be separated and redistributed by simply shaking or tapping the retort. The contents of the retort have become indivisible, "individual." This can be compared to the formation of the second body in us. The fire that brings about the fusion is produced by "friction," which is produced in us by the inner struggle between "yes" and "no." If we give in to all our desires and indulge them, no struggle will take place, no "friction," no fire. If, on the other hand, we actively struggle against the desires that prevent us from attaining a specific goal, we will create the fire necessary to eventually transform our inner world into a single whole.

Let us return to our analogy. The chemical compound or alloy obtained by fusion possesses certain qualities, such as specific gravity and electrical conductivity. Nevertheless, by means of a certain kind of work upon it, these characteristics may be enhanced; that is, the alloy may be given new properties that did not initially belong to it. It can be magnetized or made radioactive. The alloy's capacity to acquire new properties corresponds to our capacity to acquire new knowledge and strength through formation of the third body.

Once the third body has taken form and acquired all its possible knowledge and powers, the problem remains of securing them, because they could otherwise be removed by external influences just as easily as they had been acquired. These properties may be made the permanent and inalienable possession of the third body only by means of a special kind of work. The process by which these acquired properties are secured corresponds to the formation of the fourth body.

Only a person who possesses four fully developed bodies can be called "man" in the full sense of the word. This person possesses many properties that ordinary man does not possess, including *immortality* or, more correctly, *existence after death*. All religions and ancient teachings share the idea that man attains immortality by acquiring the fourth body, and they all provide indications of ways to achieve this.

INNER ALCHEMY

I N EVERYTHING WE DO, we are limited by the amount of energy produced by our organism. Every function and state, every action, thought and emotion, requires a specific expenditure of energy in the form of a specific substance. If we come to the conclusion that we must awaken and "remember ourselves," this will be possible only if we have in us the energy required for "self-remembering." We can study, understand or experience something only if we have the energy for studying, understanding or experiencing.

The human organism is like a chemical factory that has been designed to produce a very large output. But in the ordinary conditions of life the factory never reaches the full production possible because it uses only a small part of its available machinery to produce only the quantity of material that is necessary to sustain itself. It goes without saying that the factory is running inefficiently. In fact, it actually yields nothing, no product. Its machinery and elaborate equipment barely maintain its own existence and actually serve no useful purpose at all.

The work of the factory consists in processing material, transforming coarser kinds of matter (in the cosmic sense) into finer ones. The factory receives, as raw material from the outside world, a variety of coarse substances, and transforms them into finer substances by a whole series of complex *alchemical* processes. But in the ordinary conditions of life the production of the finer matters, which are important for experiencing higher states of consciousness and the functioning of higher centers, is insufficient, and they are all wasted on the maintenance of the factory itself. If we could succeed in bringing the production up to its possible maximum, we would begin to accumulate the fine material, which would saturate the whole of the body, all its cells, and gradually settle in them, crystallizing in a special way. Eventually this crystallization of the fine material would gradually bring the whole organism to a higher level, a higher plane of being.

"Learn to separate the fine from the coarse"—this principle from *The Emerald Tablet of Hermes Trismegistus* refers to the work of the "human factory." If we "learn to separate the fine from the coarse," that is, if we increase the production of fine material to its maximum capacity, we will by this very fact create the possibility of an inner growth that can be brought about by no other means. The development of the inner bodies of man is a material process analogous to the growth of the physical body. In order to grow, a child must have good food and a healthy organism to prepare the material necessary for the growth of tissues. The same is necessary for the growth of the higher bodies. All the fine substances that are required must be produced within the physical organism, and this is possible provided the human factory is working properly and economically.

All the substances necessary for maintaining the life of the organism, as well as for the higher functions of consciousness and the growth of higher bodies, are produced by the organism from the food that enters it from outside. The human organism receives three kinds of food:

1. The food we eat
2. The air we breathe
3. The impressions we receive

It is not difficult to recognize that air is a kind of food for the organism. But in what way *impressions* can represent a kind of sustenance is not at first so apparent. We must, however, keep in mind that every time we receive an impression from the outside world, whether it takes the form of sound, sight or smell, we also receive a certain amount of energy that animates us. This energy, entering the organism from outside, is matter that nourishes the organism as food in the full sense of the term.

For its normal existence the organism must receive all three kinds of food. It cannot survive on one or even on two kinds of sustenance. But the significance of these foods and the quantities required are not the same. The organism can live for a relatively long time without a supply of physical food. There are many examples of people who have starved for over sixty days, where the body lost some of its vitality but recovered quickly once they began eating again. Of course, starvation of this kind cannot be considered as complete, since in all such cases the subjects did not stop drinking water. Nevertheless, even without water a person can live for several days. Without air we can live for only a few minutes, and as a rule we will die after four minutes. Without impressions a person cannot live even for a second. If for some reason the flow of impressions were stopped, or if the organism were somehow unable to receive impressions, it would instantly die. The flow of impressions from outside is like a drive belt communicating motion to us, where the principal motor is nature, the world around us. Through our impressions, nature transmits to us the energy by which we live and move and have our being. If the inflow of this energy is arrested, our machine will immediately shut down. Impressions are therefore the most important of the three kinds of food, although, of course, no one can exist for long on impressions alone. We can live for a little while on impressions and air. With all three kinds of food the organism can live to the end of its normal life span and produce the substances necessary not only for maintaining life, but also for the creation and growth of higher bodies.

If we understand the concept of scale and levels of materiality, it is possible to examine the relation between man's functions and the planes of the universe, and to clearly establish the reasons for the differences between the centers. The centers work with substances of different materiality. The center working with a more coarse, heavy, dense material works more slowly. The center working with a lighter, more mobile material works more quickly. This constitutes their principal difference.

As we have seen, the thinking center is the slowest of the three lower centers. The moving center works faster with a substance that is many times lighter and more mobile. The thinking center is never able to follow the functioning of the moving center. We are unable to follow either our own movements or those of another person unless they are artificially slowed down, and we are even less capable of following work of the internal, instinctive functions of our organism. The feeling center can work with an even lighter material. But in practice it very rarely does so, and most of the time its work differs little in intensity and speed from that of the moving center.

As noted above, our human machine has two higher centers, fully developed and properly functioning but not connected with the three centers in which we are aware of ourselves. These are the higher feeling center and the higher thinking center, each working with the finest substances. If we consider the human machine in terms of the materials used by the centers, it should become clear why differences in quality preclude a connection with the higher centers. The thinking center works with the heavier substance, and the moving center with a less dense substance. If the feeling center were to use the even finer substance for which it is designed, its functioning would be connected with that of the higher feeling center. In fact, in cases where the feeling center reaches the intensity that is given by this finer substance, a temporary connection with the higher feeling center takes place, and a person experiences new emotions and impressions that are unlike any he has known before, for which he has no words to describe. But ordinarily the difference in speed between our usual feelings and the higher feelings is so great that no connection can take place. We remain deaf to the voices that are speaking and *calling to us* from the higher feeling center.

The higher thinking center, working with an even lighter substance, is still further removed and inaccessible. Connection is possible only through the higher feeling center, and it occurs so rarely that the only examples we know of are from descriptions of mystical experiences and ecstatic states. These states can occur through religious emotions, pathological experiences such as epileptic fits, or traumatic brain injuries, or, for very brief moments, through narcotics or other drugs.

In order to obtain a correct, permanent connection with the higher centers, it is necessary to regulate the lower centers and make them work faster. Unfortunately, the lower centers often work in a wrong way, shirking their own proper functions and taking on themselves those that should belong to other centers. This considerably slows down the entire machine and makes acceleration of the centers very difficult. Therefore, in order to regulate and accelerate the lower centers, we must first free each one from those functions that do not belong to it, and redirect its work to the functioning that it is best equipped to handle.

If we wish to regulate the three centers whose functions constitute our life, we must learn to economize the energy produced by our organism, that is, to not waste it on unnecessary functions but save it for the activity that will eventually lead to a connection between the lower and the higher centers. All work on oneself, on the formation of inner unity, pursues the same ultimate goal. What one system calls the "astral body" another designates the "higher feeling center," although there is more to this distinction than terminology alone. These are, more correctly, different aspects of the next stage of man's evolution. It can be said that the "astral body" is a prerequisite for the "higher feeling center" to function in unison with the lower, or that the "higher feeling center" is a prerequisite for the development of the "astral body." The "mental body," on the other hand, corresponds to the "higher thinking center." They are not the same thing, but one requires the other, one cannot exist without the other, and one is the expression of certain aspects and functions of the other. In the highest stage of unity, the fourth body requires the complete and harmonious working of all of the centers, and implies, or is rather the expression of, complete control over this working.

What is necessary to understand is that all intellectual, emotional, volitional and other internal processes are completely material, including the most exalted poetic and religious inspirations, and mystical revelations. All psychic processes are material, and all depend upon the quality of the material or substance used. There is not a single process that does not require the expenditure of a certain corresponding substance. If this material is present, the process continues and when the substance is exhausted, the process comes to a stop.

III

WORLDS
WITHIN WORLDS

INSIDE THE MILKY WAY

I T IS IMPOSSIBLE TO STUDY man without also studying the universe. We are a microcosm of the world we inhabit. We were created according to the same laws that governed the creation of the world. By knowing and understanding ourselves, we will know and understand the world at large, as well as the laws that govern it and us. The study of the world and the study of oneself must therefore run parallel, with each helping the other.

In relation to the term "world," we need to recognize from the outset that there are actually many worlds, and that we live not in one but in several at the same time. This concept can be difficult to understand because in our ordinary language the term "world" is typically used in the singular. We employ the plural "worlds" only to emphasize the same basic concept, that is, to express the idea of various worlds existing parallel to one another, not of worlds existing *one within another.* But the fact of the matter is that we live in various worlds that contain one another and to which we stand in different relations.

In seeking to understand the worlds in which we live, we must first ask ourselves what we call "world" in the sense most immediately relevant to us. The answer is that we most often are referring to the world of people in which we live, the human world of which we are a part. Yet humanity is also an inextricable component of organic life of the earth. Therefore, it would be more accurate to say that the world most relevant to us is *organic life on earth,* the world of plants, animals and people.

But organic life is also in a world. What then is "world" for organic life? To this we can answer that for organic life our planet the earth is "world," the terrestrial globe, or rather the surface of the terrestrial globe.

But the earth is also in a world. What then is "world" from the perspective of the earth? Looking at the relation of the earth to the universe, we see that as one of the small planets revolving around the sun, the earth is a component part of the planetary world of the solar system. The mass of the earth forms an almost negligible fraction compared with the whole mass of planets, and the planets exert a great influence on the life of the earth and on all living organisms—a far greater influence than our science imagines. The life of individual people, of collective groups, of humanity, depends upon planetary influences in many ways. "World" for the earth is the planetary world of the solar system, of which it forms a part.

What is "world" for all the planets taken together? The planets also live, as we live upon the earth. But the planetary world in its turn participates in the solar system, and does so as a very unimportant part because the mass of all the planets taken together is many times less than the mass of the sun. "World" for the planets is the sun, or, rather, the sphere of the sun's influence or solar system, of which the planets form a part.

For the sun, in turn, "world" is the galaxy of stars, the Milky Way, in which it is but one of a vast number of suns and solar systems. Furthermore, from an astronomical point of view, it is quite possible to presume a multitude of galaxies beyond our own, existing at enormous distances from one another in the space of "all galaxies." Taken together, these galaxies will be "world" for the Milky Way.

Science cannot look further, but philosophical thought will see the ultimate principle lying beyond all the galaxies—that is, the Absolute, known in Hindu terminology as Brahman. This *Whole*, or *One* or *All*, is "world" for "all worlds." Logically it is quite possible to conceive of a state of things where everything—All—forms one single "Whole." This "Whole" would by definition be an autonomous "Absolute" because, as the unification of all things, it would be infinite and indivisible, and not dependent upon anything. The Absolute—that is, the state where all things constitute a unified Whole—is the primordial state of the universe, from which the diversity of the phenomena arises by division and differentiation.

We live in all these worlds simultaneously but in different ways. More precisely, we are first and foremost influenced by the world closest to us, the one we are a part of. More distant worlds also influence us, directly as well as through other intermediate worlds, but their action is diminished the further they are from us. The *direct* influence of the Absolute does not reach us. But the influence of the next world and the influence of the starry world clearly affect our lives, although they are certainly unknown to science.

THE LAW OF THREE FORCES

I N THE PARALLEL STUDY of the world and of man, we can assume that the same laws pertain everywhere and in everything. At the same time, some laws are easier to observe in the world, and others easier to observe in man. In certain cases it is better to begin with the world and then move on to man, and in others it is better to begin with man and move on to the world.

This study of the world and of man demonstrates the fundamental unity of all things and helps us find analogies in phenomena of different orders. All the processes at work in man and the world are governed by a very small number of fundamental laws. All the apparent variety we see around us is in fact the product of a few basic forces operating in different numerical combinations. In order to understand the mechanics of the universe, we must first learn to resolve complex phenomena into the basic forces of which they are composed.

The first fundamental law is the law of *three principles* or *three forces,* which determines unity and diversity throughout the universe. According to this law, which is often called the "Law of Three," every phenomenon, on whatever scale and in whatever world it may appear, from molecular to cosmic, is the result of the interaction of three different and opposing forces. Contemporary thought recognizes the existence and necessity of two forces to produce a phenomenon: force and resistance, positive and negative polarity, positive and negative currents and so on. But this view does not envision two forces in every phenomenon, nor has it so much as acknowledged the possibility of a third constituent force.

According to ancient science, one or two forces are insufficient to produce a phenomenon. A third force must be present, without which the first two can never produce anything whatsoever. This teaching of *three forces* is at the foundation of all ancient systems. The first force may be called "active" or "positive"; the second, "passive" or "negative"; the third, "neutralizing." But these are *merely names* and, in fact, all three forces are equally active. They appear as active, passive or neutralizing only at the point of their intersection; that is, they adopt these functions *only in relation to one another and only at a given moment in time.* We are more or less able to comprehend the first two forces, and the third is occasionally observable at the point of application of the forces, or in the "medium" or the "result." But, in general, the third force is not something we can typically observe or understand. This is because of the fundamental limitations of our ordinary psychological activity and the fundamental categories of our limited perception of the phenomenal world, that is, our perception of space and time. We can no more directly perceive the third force in action than we can spatially perceive the "fourth dimension."

Nevertheless, it is possible to learn to observe the action of the three forces within us by studying ourselves—the manifestation of our thought, our consciousness, our habits and desires. Let us suppose, for instance, that we decide to work on ourselves in order to attain a higher level of being. In this case, our desire, our initiative, is the active force, whereas the inertia of all our habitual psychological life, which opposes the initiative, will be the passive or negative force. In the end, either these two forces will balance each other out, or one will completely conquer the other, although, at the same time, becoming too weak for any further action. Thus the two forces will, as it were, revolve one around the other, with one eventually absorbing the other and producing no result whatever. This stalemate may endure over the course of our entire lives. We may feel desire and initiative, but it all may be absorbed in the struggle to overcome the habitual inertia of life, leaving nothing in the end to pursue the worthy goal of our original decision. And so the process may go on until the third force makes its appearance, perhaps, in the form of *new knowledge* that shows the advantage, or rather the necessity, of work on ourselves and, in this way, reinforces the initiative. Then, thanks to the support of this third force, the initiative may be able to overcome the inertia and we can become active in the desired direction.

We can find other examples of the three forces, including the eventual appearance of the third force, in all manifestations of our psychic life, in all phenomena of communal life and of humanity as a whole, as well as of nature around us. For now, however, it will be sufficient to understand the general principle that every phenomenon, of whatever magnitude, inevitably represents the manifestation of three forces and cannot be produced by one or two forces. Whenever we observe an action grinding to a halt or endlessly hesitating, we can say that, at the given point, the third force is lacking. At the same time, a phenomenon that appears to be simple may actually be very complicated, consisting of a complex combination of trinities. More important, it must be remembered that we cannot directly apprehend phenomena as manifestations of three forces because we cannot observe the objective world in our subjective state of consciousness. The subjective or phenomenal world of our observation is incomplete, only relatively real, because we see in phenomena only the manifestation of one or two forces. If we could see the manifestation of three forces in every action, we would then see the world *as it is* (things in themselves). The third force is a property of the real world.

THE RAY OF CREATION

Referring to the Law of Three, we may now say that in the Absolute and in everything else there are three forces at play—the active, the passive and the neutralizing. Since by definition the Absolute represents a unified whole, the three forces in it must also be united as one whole. Moreover, in forming a unified, independent whole, the three forces possess an independent will, as well as full consciousness and complete understanding of their own nature and function. The concept of the unity of the three forces in the Absolute forms the basis of many ancient teachings, including the consubstantial and indivisible Trinity of Christianity, and the Trimurti of Brahma, Vishnu and Shiva in Hinduism.

The three forces of the Absolute purposefully separate and combine, and at the points of junction create phenomena, or second-tier "worlds." These worlds, created by the will of the Absolute, depend entirely upon this will in every aspect of their existence. In each of them the three forces again act. Since, however, each then represents only a part and not the whole of the Absolute, the three forces in it do not form a single whole. Outside of the Absolute, the three forces involve three wills, consciousnesses and unities. Each of the three forces carries within itself the potential to function in the capacity of the other two, but at their meeting point manifests only one principle—the active, the passive or the neutralizing. It is at these points that they combine to form a trinity that produces a world of the second tier, which is subject to the action of three forces.

The three divided forces in a second-tier world, meeting together, create new worlds of the third order, in which the number of forces will be six. Within these worlds are created worlds of a new order in which twelve forces act, followed by worlds within worlds governed by twenty-four, forty-eight and ninety-six forces, and so on. We will designate the worlds by the number of forces acting within them.

The Absolute gives birth to a potentially infinite number of second-tier worlds, each of which contains the beginning of a chain of worlds in what we shall call a "ray of creation." If we take one of these second-tier worlds, designated "world 3" because it has three forces, it will be the world that represents all the starry worlds or galaxies in the universe. Only one of these, however, is relevant to us, namely, the Milky Way, designated as "world 6." And of the various suns that comprise the Milky Way, we are concerned only with our own sun as "world 12," upon which we directly depend. Within the solar system the planetary world is the most relevant as "world 24," of which the planet earth as "world 48" is the most immediate. The end of our ray of creation is the moon as "world 96." This chain of worlds in which we exist—that is, from our perspective, the "world" in the broadest sense of the term—can be represented as shown in the diagram below.

The number of forces in each world—1, 3, 6, 12 and so on—indicates the number of laws that govern the given world. The fewer the laws it is subject to, the closer the world is to the will of the Absolute. The more laws there are in it, the further the world is from the will of the Absolute, and the more mechanical it is. Our world of the earth, "world 48," is subject to no less than forty-eight orders of laws, that is to say, very far from the will of the Absolute and in a remote and dark corner of the universe.

The idea of the ray of creation can be found throughout ancient teachings and, in fact, many of the naive geocentric conceptions of the universe known to us are either incomplete expositions of this idea or distortions due to literal understanding. The development of the ray from the Absolute contradicts some modern views. Take, for instance, the continuum of sun, earth and moon. According to the

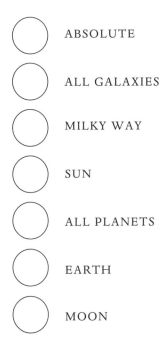

ABSOLUTE

ALL GALAXIES

MILKY WAY

SUN

ALL PLANETS

EARTH

MOON

usual understanding, the moon is a cold, dead celestial body that once resembled the earth, that is, it used to have a molten core and prior to that was a gaseous mass like the sun. According to this view, the earth was also once like the sun, but it too has gradually cooled down and will one day become a cold mass like the moon. It is usually assumed that the sun is also cooling down and will eventually come to resemble first the earth, then the moon. The idea of the ray of creation and its growth from the Absolute conflicts with these general views, and instead regards the moon as a planet that is being born. It is slowly growing warmer, and in time (given a favorable development of the ray of creation) it will come to resemble the earth, eventually developing a satellite of its own. This new moon will represent a new link in the ray of creation. By the same token, the earth is not cooling but actually growing warmer, and may in time come to resemble the sun. An example of this phenomenon can be found in the system of Jupiter, which serves as a sun for its satellites.

As noted above, the will of the Absolute is manifested only in world 3, the world that it has directly created immediately within itself. Its unmitigated will does not reach world 6, but is manifested there only in the form of mechanical laws. Further on, in worlds 12, 24, 48 and 96, the will of the Absolute is even more remote and even further mediated. We might say that in world 3 the Absolute creates a general plan or outline for the rest of the universe, which is then filled in mechanically. The will of the Absolute can be felt in subsequent worlds only as the mechanical realization of this plan. This means that if the Absolute wanted to manifest its will directly in our world (which would conflict with the mechanical laws that pertain here), it would first have to destroy all the intermediate worlds between it and our world. The concept of a miracle, in the sense of "violating ordinary physical laws by the Will that established them," not only violates common sense but is contrary to the very idea of Will itself. Thus, in reality a "miracle" can only be a manifestation of laws that are unknown or unfamiliar to us, or, to put it another way, the manifestation in our world of the laws of another world.

Here on earth we are very far removed from the will of the Absolute, separated by forty-eight orders of mechanical laws and, in our mechanical life, subject to the influence of the moon. If, however, we could free ourselves from half of these laws, we would then be subject to only twenty-four orders of laws, that is, to those of the planetary world, which would bring us one stage closer to the Absolute and its will. If we could then free ourselves from half of the remaining laws, we would be subject only to the twelve orders of laws of the sun, and therefore another stage closer to the Absolute. If, again, we could free ourselves from half of these laws, we would be subject only to the laws of the galaxy and thus separated by only a single stage from the unmitigated will of the Absolute. And this possibility of gradual liberation from mechanical laws exists for us. If we develop consciousness and will in ourselves, and subject our mechanical manifestations to them, we will escape from the power of the moon.

THE LAW OF OCTAVES

T HE SECOND FUNDAMENTAL LAW of the universe is the Law of Octaves, often called the "Law of Seven." In order to understand this law, it is necessary to regard the universe as *consisting of vibrations*. These vibrations occur in all kinds of matter that make up the universe, from the finest to the coarsest. They issue from various sources and proceed in various directions, crisscrossing, colliding, growing stronger or weaker, stopping one another and so on.

At the base of the understanding of vibrations, ancient science recognizes the basic principle of their *discontinuity*—that is, the definite and necessary characteristic of all vibrations in nature, whether of increasing or decreasing frequency, to develop not as even, continuous, uniform oscillations but with periodic accelerations and retardations in speed. According to this principle, the force of the original impulse does not act uniformly in vibrations but, as it were, is sometimes stronger, sometimes weaker.

The laws that govern the slowing down or the deflection of vibrations were known to ancient science and incorporated into a particular formula that has been preserved up to our time. In this formula the period in which vibrations are doubled is divided into *eight* unequal steps corresponding to the rate of increase in the vibrations. The eighth step repeats the first step with double the number of vibrations. This period of doubling between a given number and twice that number is called an *octave*, that is to say, *composed of eight*.

This formula represents the form in which the concept of the octave has been handed down from teacher to pupil, and from one school to another. A long, long time ago one of these schools discovered that it was possible to apply this formula to music. In this way they obtained our diatonic musical scale—*do-re-mi-fa-sol-la-si-do*—which was known in the most distant antiquity, then forgotten, and then discovered or "reinvented" again. The structure of the seven-tone scale, with semitones missing at the intervals *mi-fa* and *si-do,* gives a scheme of the cosmic law of "intervals," or absent semitones. In this respect when octaves are spoken of in a cosmic or a mechanical sense, only the half-steps between *mi-fa* and *si-do* are called "intervals."

The diatonic scale thus represents the formula of the Law of Octaves that was first developed in ancient schools, then applied to music. At the same time, however, if we study the law's manifestations in other, nonmusical kinds of vibrations, we shall see that laws are everywhere the same, and that the vibrations intrinsic to light, heat, chemical reactions and magnetism are subject to the same principles as sound. For instance, physics knows of the light scale, and in chemistry the periodic system of the elements is closely related to the principle of octaves. Our division of time, that is, our separation of the days of the week into workdays and Sundays, reflects the general law that governs our activity. And the biblical myth of creation, in which God created the world in six days and rested on the seventh, is an expression or at least an indication of this law, though incomplete.

If we grasp its true significance, the Law of Octaves provides us with an entirely new explanation of the whole of life and the development of phenomena on every plane of the universe. This law explains, for example, why there are no straight lines in nature. It also explains why we cannot "do," why with us everything is "done," and usually in a way opposed to what we want or expect. Whenever we set out to do something, we always end up doing something different, all the while thinking that we are doing just what we originally intended. All of this is the direct effect of the "intervals" or decreases in the frequency of vibrations as they develop.

So far we have focused on the discontinuity of vibrations and the way forces can deviate. There are also two other principles that we must try to grasp: first, that either ascent or descent is inevitable in every line of development, and second, that in every line, whether ascending or descending, there are periodic fluctuations, that is, rises and falls. Development implies change, and ascent or descent is the inevitable cosmic condition of any action. We do not see or understand what is going on around and within us. This is because we continually think that things can remain at the same level for a long time, and we do not allow for the inevitability of descent when there is no ascent. We also take descent to be ascent, not realizing that *ascents* where we imagine them are in fact impossible, as, for example, it is impossible to increase consciousness by mechanical means.

After distinguishing ascending and descending octaves in the world around us, we must learn to distinguish ascent and descent within the octaves themselves. Whatever the aspect of our life, nothing ever remains level and constant. Everywhere and in everything the pendulum swings, waves rise and fall. Consider our energy which suddenly increases and then, just as suddenly, weakens; our moods which "become better" or "become worse" without any visible reason; our feelings, our desires, our intentions, our decisions. All these are continually ascending or descending, becoming stronger or weaker.

Observations based on the Law of Octaves show that "vibrations" can develop in various ways. If an octave is interrupted, the vibrations can be seen as merely beginning, then falling, or as being swallowed up by other, stronger vibrations that intersect or go in an opposite direction. If an octave deviates from the original direction, the vibrations change in nature and give results contrary to what was originally expected. It is only in octaves of a cosmic order, whether descending or ascending, that vibrations develop in a consecutive and orderly way, and continue in the same direction in which they started.

Further observations show that octaves have the potential to develop consistently in life, both in nature and even human activity, although this kind of development is rare and then often based on what looks to be an *accident*. What sometimes happens is that, as the octave progresses, other octaves, running parallel to, intersecting or meeting it, in some way or other *fill up its* "*intervals*" so that its vibrations can continue their development unchecked. At the moment the given octave passes through an "interval," there enters an "additional shock" that corresponds in force and character. This allows the octave to develop further along the original direction without any loss or change in the nature of its vibrations. But in such cases there is an essential difference between ascending and descending octaves.

In an ascending octave, the first "interval" comes after the third note, between *mi* and *fa*. If corresponding additional energy enters at this point, the octave will develop without hindrance up to *si*, the seventh note. But in order to continue through the interval between *si* and *do,* it needs a *much stronger "additional shock."* At this point the vibrations are of a much higher pitch, and so require greater intensity to prevent the octave's development from being slowed. In a descending octave, on the other hand, the most difficult "interval" occurs at the very beginning, immediately after the first *do*, and the material to fill it is very often found either in *do* itself or in the lateral vibrations induced by *do*. This is why a descending octave develops much more easily than an ascending octave, and in passing beyond *si* it reaches *fa,* the fifth note, without hindrance. Here an "additional shock" is necessary, though *considerably less strong* than the first shock between *do* and *si*.

In the operation of the Law of Octaves, there are, in their relation to each other, *fundamental* and *subordinate* octaves. The fundamental octave is like the trunk of a tree giving off branches of lateral octaves. The seven fundamental notes and the two "intervals," *the bearers of new directions,* give altogether nine links of a chain, three groups of three links each. The formation of octaves, and the relation of subordinate octaves of different orders, can be compared with the formation of a tree. From the basic trunk come major branches on all sides, which split in turn into lesser branches, which become smaller and smaller, and finally are covered with leaves. The process continues on a smaller scale in the formation of the leaves, of the veins and serrations.

The complete example of the Law of Octaves can be seen in the great cosmic octave in the ray of creation that reaches us. The ray be-

gins with the Absolute, which is the *All*. This *All*, which possesses complete unity, will and consciousness, creates worlds within itself, thereby
beginning the *descending* world octave of which the Absolute is the *do*.
The worlds the Absolute creates within itself are thus *si*, with the "interval" between *do* and *si* being filled by the *will of the Absolute*. The
creative process develops further under the impetus of the original impulse with the assistance of the "additional shock." *Si* passes into *la*,
which from our perspective is our star galaxy, the Milky Way. *La* passes
into *sol*—our sun, the solar system—and *sol* passes into *fa*—the world
of the planets of our solar system. And here, between the planetary
world as a whole and our earth, occurs an "interval." The consequence
of this interval is that the planetary emanations carrying various influences to the earth cannot reach it, or, more correctly, the earth, rather
than receiving, reflects them. At this point, in order to fill the "interval,"
a special device has been created for receiving and transmitting these
planetary influences. This device is *organic life on earth,* which transmits
to the earth all of the influences intended for it. This makes possible the
further development and growth of the earth, *mi* of the cosmic octave;
and then of the moon, or *re*; after which follows another *do*—*Nothing*.
The ray of creation thus extends from *All* to *Nothing*.

In the cosmic octave the sun originally sounds as *sol*, but begins
at a certain moment also to sound as *do* in a new descending octave.
Proceeding to the level of the planets, this new octave passes into *si*
and, descending still lower, it produces three notes, *la, sol, fa*, which
create and constitute all of the earth's organic life as we know it. *Mi* of
this octave blends with *mi* of the cosmic octave, that is, with *the earth*,
and *re* of this octave blends with *re* of the cosmic octave, that is, with
the moon. Organic life functions as the earth's organ of both perception
and emanation. At every moment, by way of organic life, each portion
of the earth's surface sends emanations toward the sun, the planets and
the moon, which each require a specific kind of emanation. Everything
that happens on earth creates emanations, and many events *occur* just
because certain kinds of emanations are required from a certain place
on the earth's surface. The two octaves can be illustrated as follows:

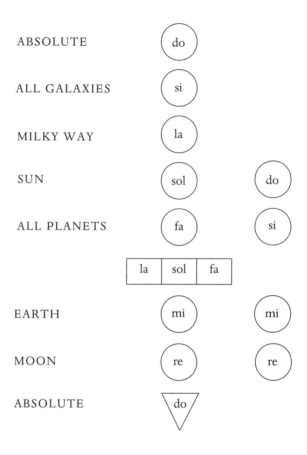

Passing from the universe to the study of man, we must try to understand the idea of "additional shocks" that enable the lines of forces to reach a projected aim. As suggested above, shocks may occur accidentally. By chance our activities may happen to fall into and move along some channel or other that has been carved out by cosmic or mechanical forces, creating the illusion that some kind of aim is being attained. Such accidental correspondence between results and the aims we have set for ourselves, or the attainment of aims in small things *that can have no consequences,* gives rise to the conviction that we are able to attain any aim, that we can "conquer nature," "arrange the whole of our life"

and so on. As a matter of fact, of course, we are unable to do any such thing because, not only have we no control over what happens outside ourselves, but we have no control even over what happens within ourselves. This last must be clearly understood. At the same time we must understand that control over things begins with control over things in oneself, *with control over oneself.* A person who cannot control himself, or the course of things within himself, can control nothing.

The technical part of this control is explained by the Law of Octaves. As we have seen, octaves can develop in the desired direction only if "additional shocks" enter at the right moments, that is, at the points where vibrations slow down. If "additional shocks" do not enter at these moments, octaves change their direction. Of course, one can hardly expect such "shocks" to show up accidentally all by themselves at just the right time. For each of us there remains a choice among three approaches to life. We can perhaps find a direction for our activities that corresponds to the mechanical line of events of a given moment, in other words "go where the wind blows" or "swim with the stream," even if this contradicts our inner inclinations, convictions and sympathies. We can reconcile ourselves to the failure of everything we start out to do. Or, we can learn to recognize the "intervals" in the lines of our activity and to *create* the "additional shocks" we need, in other words, learn to apply to our own activities the method used by cosmic forces at the necessary moments.

In trying to understand the Law of Octaves, it is important to avoid too much theorizing. We have to understand and feel this law in ourselves. Only then will we be able to see it operating outside ourselves.

DEGREES OF MATERIALITY

I N THE UNIVERSE in the form of the ray of creation, everything can be weighed and measured, up to and including the Absolute. The Absolute is as material, and thus as physically quantifiable, as the moon or a human being. If the Absolute can be called "God," this means that God can be weighed and measured. But the concept of "materiality" is as relative as any other. In the ray of creation there are seven planes in the universe, seven worlds, one within another, and everything that refers to the world is also divided into seven corresponding categories. The materiality of the Absolute is of an order different from that of "all galaxies," which is of an order different from the Milky Way. The materiality, in each case, of the Milky Way, "all planets," the earth and the moon is of an order different from the materiality of the worlds below. This concept is at first difficult to grasp because we are so used to the assumption that all matter is basically the same. This assumption actually serves as the basis for all of physics, astrophysics and chemistry. And it is indeed the case that all matter is the same. But *materiality* varies, and has different degrees depending upon the characteristics of the energy manifested at a given point.

Matter or substance necessarily presupposes the existence of force and energy. But this does not imply a dualistic conception of the world, because the concepts of matter and force are just as relative as any other. For example, in the Absolute, where all is one, matter and force are also one. In this case, however, matter and force are not to be un-

74

derstood as principles of the real world in itself but rather as properties or characteristics of the phenomenal world insofar as it is observed by us. All we need to begin study of the universe is an elementary understanding of matter and energy such as we get by ordinary sensory perception, taking matter as the "constant" and "changes" in the state of matter as manifestations of force or energy. These changes can in turn be understood as the result of vibrations that begin in the center, that is, in the Absolute, before radiating outward like waves in all directions, crisscrossing, colliding, and merging, until they come to a stop at the end of the ray of creation. From this point of view, the world consists of vibrations and matter, or, if you prefer, of matter in a state of vibration, that is, vibrating matter. The rate of vibration is inversely proportional to the density of matter. In the Absolute, vibrations are the most rapid, and matter is the least dense. In the next world, vibrations are slower and matter is denser. The further from the Absolute, the slower the vibrations and the denser the matter.

"Matter" may be regarded as made up of "atoms," defined as the result of the smallest possible division of such matter. In every order of matter, there is a point beyond which such matter can no longer be divided in the world in question, a point that represents the size of the atoms making up such world's materiality. Only the atoms in the world of the Absolute are truly indivisible. The atoms of the next world, that is, world 3, consist of three atoms that correspond to the world of the Absolute, and are three times larger, three times denser and three times slower than those of the Absolute. The atoms of world 6 consist of six atoms of the Absolute combined, albeit as a single atom, and the atoms of the next worlds consist of twelve, twenty-four, forty-eight and ninety-six primordial particles. The atoms of world 96 are enormous compared with the atoms of world 1, and are correspondingly slower and denser.

The seven worlds of the ray of creation represent seven different orders of materiality, and instead of one concept of matter, we have seven different kinds of matter. But our ordinary conception of materiality is ill-suited to understand the materiality of worlds 96 and 48.

From the scientific perspective, the matter of world 24 is so rarefied that it is essentially hypothetical, to say nothing of the still finer matter of world 12, which is not even matter. Since these matters correspond to the various orders making up the universe, they are not separated into layers but interpenetrate one another, just as more familiar kinds of matter of different densities sometimes become intermingled. For example, a piece of wood can become saturated with water, and water can be saturated with gas. Exactly the same relation occurs among the different kinds of matter that make up the universe, with the finer permeating the coarser, although, as noted, matter of higher planes is not material at all in the lower planes.

All of the matter making up our world—the food we eat, the water we drink, the air we breathe, the stones we use to build our houses, and our own bodies—everything is permeated by all the various matters that exist in the universe. There is therefore no need to study the sun in order to discover the matter of the solar world. It can be found within us, included as the result of the division of our own atoms. In the same way, we have within us all the various matters of the other worlds. Each of us is, in the full sense of the term, a universe in miniature, a "microcosm," including in ourselves all the matters making up the universe, and operating under the same forces and laws that govern the universe. In studying oneself, therefore, we can study the whole world, just as in studying the world we can study oneself. But a complete parallel between man and the world can only be drawn if we take "man" in the full sense of the word, that is, a person whose latent powers are developed. Someone who remains undeveloped, or who has not completed the course of his possible evolution, cannot be taken to represent a microcosm of the universe; this person is actually more like an unfinished world.

As noted above, the study of oneself must progress hand in hand with the study of the fundamental laws of the universe, which are the same on every plane. Returning to the Law of Three, we must learn to find the manifestations of it in everything we study and in all our actions. Discovering its application in any sphere of activity will immediately reveal to us a great store of new knowledge, much of which we did not see before. Ordinary chemistry, for example, is ignorant of the Law of Three and studies matter without taking its cosmic properties into account. There is, however, another kind of chemistry, a special chemistry or "alchemy," if you will, that takes into consideration cosmic properties of each substance that are determined *by its place* and *by the force acting through it* at a given moment. Two substances in the same place can often differ greatly depending on the force manifested through them. Each substance can be the conductor of any one of the three forces and thus be *active, passive or neutralizing.* And it can be none of these if no force is manifesting through it at the given moment, or if it is taken without relation to the manifestation of forces. Every substance can thus appear, as it were, in one of four different aspects or states. In this connection it must be noted that when we talk about matter, we are not speaking of its chemical elements. This special chemistry looks upon every substance, even the most complex, as itself functioning separately as an "element." This is the only way to study cosmic properties, because all complex compounds have their own cosmic role and function. From this point of view, an "atom" of a given substance is redefined as the smallest amount of such substance that retains all of its chemical, physical, and cosmic properties. Of course, atoms of different substances will thus vary in size, and in some cases an atom may even be visible to the naked eye.

Distinguishing degrees of materiality allows us to examine the relation between man's functions and the planes of the universe. The principal difference between the centers is that they work with substances of different materiality. The thinking center is the slowest of the three lower centers, operating with a substance on the level of world 48. The moving center works faster with a substance of world 24 that is many times lighter and more mobile. The feeling center can work with a substance of world 12, an even lighter material, although in practice it very rarely does so. The higher feeling center works with a substance of world 12, and the higher thinking center with a substance of world 6. As discussed above, the different degrees of materiality explain why the higher centers cannot be connected with the lower. In order to obtain a correct and invariable connection between the lower and the higher centers, it is necessary to regulate and quicken the work of the lower centers.

In terms of the Law of Octaves, man serves as an apparatus in the possible evolution of substances, which enter the organism as three kinds of food. The first kind is what is usually called food—for example, bread—which enters as *do* and has the possibility of passing into *re* in the stomach, where the substances change their vibrations and density. These substances are transformed chemically, become mixed, and by means of certain combinations pass into *re,* which also has the possibility of passing into *mi.* But *mi* cannot evolve by itself. Here the second kind of food—that is, air—comes to its assistance, entering as *do* of a second octave. It helps *mi* of the first octave to pass into *fa,* after which its evolution can proceed further. In its turn, at a similar point, the second octave also requires help from a higher octave, which comes in the form of the third kind of food—that is, impressions—which enters as *do* of the third octave. Thus the first octave evolves up to *si,* which is the finest substance that our human organism can produce from what is usually called food. The evolution of a piece of bread reaches this level of materiality but cannot develop further in ordinary man. If *si* could develop and pass into *do* of a new octave, it would be possible to build a new body within ourselves. This requires special conditions, special inner combinations.

IV

THE POSSIBILITY
OF EVOLUTION

CONSCIOUS EVOLUTION

A LWAYS AND EVERYWHERE there is affirmation and negation, not only in individuals but in the whole of mankind as well. This is a mechanical law and cannot be otherwise. It operates everywhere and on every scale—in the world, in cities, in families, in the inner life of an individual. One part affirms, another denies. This is an objective law, and everyone is a slave to it. Only those who stand in the middle are free. If we can do this, we escape from this general law. But how to escape? It is very difficult. We are not strong enough, so we submit. We are weak, we are slaves. Yet the possibility exists to get free if we try slowly, gradually but steadily. From an objective point of view, of course, this means to go against this law, against nature. We can do so because a law of a different order exists; we have been given another law by God.

What is necessary to achieve freedom? Let us take the apparent opposition between science and religion. What one affirms the other denies, and vice versa. I reflect deeply on this question, reasoning as follows.

I am an insignificant man. I have only lived for fifty years, while religion has existed for thousands of years. Thousands of people have studied these religions, and yet I deny them. I ask myself: "Is it possible that they were all fools and that only I am clever?" The situation is the same with science. It also has existed for thousands of years. Suppose I deny it. The same question arises: "Can it be that I alone am more clever than all those who have studied science for so long a time?" If I reason impartially, I will recognize that I may be more intelligent than one or two others but not a thousand. If I am a normal person and I reason without bias, I will understand that I cannot be more intelligent than millions. I repeat, I am but an insignificant individual. How can I dismiss religion and science? What then is possible?

I begin to think that perhaps there is some truth in both. It is impossible for everyone to be mistaken. So I set myself the task of trying to understand the contradiction. When I begin to think and study impartially, I find that religion and science are both right, in spite of the fact that they are opposed to one another. I discover a small difference. One side takes one subject, the other side, another. Or, they study the same subject but from different angles. Or, one studies the causes, the other the effects of the same phenomenon. And so they never meet. But both are right, for both are based on laws that are rationally sound. If we take only the result, we shall never understand where the difference lies.

At a certain point both science and religion are concerned with human development, that is, the question of evolution, of change of being. Man contains this possibility within him. But it is important to understand from the beginning that evolution is, in a sense, against the general law. The evolution of a person is thus for the individual himself, the development of his own capacities to free himself from dependence on outside influences. Only this kind of development, this kind of growth, represents the *real* evolution of humanity. Apart from it there can be no evolution at all. In fact, humanity as a whole does not progress or evolve. What seems to be progress or evolution is nothing more than a superficial modification that can at any time be counterbalanced by corresponding modifications in the opposite direction.

In order to understand the law of man's possible evolution, we must first understand that, at least as far as nature is concerned, there is no need for this evolution beyond a certain point. More exactly, the evolution of humanity corresponds to the evolution of the planet, but the planet evolves according to temporal cycles that, from our perspective, are so long as to seem infinite. The greatest length of time we can possibly imagine is still too short for substantial changes to take place in the life of the planet and, consequently, in the life of humanity.

Like all other organic life, humanity exists on the earth to fulfill the needs and purposes of the planet, and is exactly as it should be for the earth's requirements at the present time. Only thought as theoretical and divorced from reality as contemporary Western thought could have come up with the idea that humanity evolves *separately from nature,* that human evolution can be understood as a gradual *conquest of nature.* This is completely impossible. We serve the ends of nature equally in living and dying, evolving and devolving—or, more exactly, nature makes use of us in the same way it utilizes the other products of evolution and devolution, albeit perhaps for different purposes. At the same time, humanity *as a whole* can never separate itself from nature, for, even as we struggle against it, we never cease to serve its ends. In fact, the evolution of humanity as a whole, or the development of these possibilities in a large number of people, not only is unnecessary for the purposes of the earth and the planetary world, but would actually be harmful or even fatal, for instance, for the moon.

Nevertheless, the potential for evolution does exist, and may be realized in *separate individuals* with the help of appropriate knowledge and methods. Since this can only serve the interests of the person himself, it runs counter to the interests, so to speak, of the planetary world. Each of us must understand this: one's evolution is necessary only to oneself. No one else has any interest in it, nor is anyone obliged to help us. On the contrary, the forces that oppose the evolution of large numbers of humanity also oppose the evolution of individuals. A person must be shrewd and outwit them. And *one person* can outwit them; *humanity* cannot. It will be clear later that these obstacles are useful to us, and would have to be intentionally created if they did not exist. It is by overcoming obstacles that we can develop the qualities we need.

This is the crux of the correct view of human evolution. There is no such thing as inevitable, mechanical evolution. Evolution occurs as the result of conscious struggle. Nature has no need or desire for this kind of evolution, and actually struggles against it. Evolution can be necessary only to ourselves when we come to understand our situation and the possibility of changing it, when we realize that we have untapped powers and unrealized treasure. Evolution is possible for the individual in the sense of attaining these powers and treasure. But if everyone, or even most people, were to realize this and desire to obtain their birthright, evolution would cease to be possible.

The individual person is so tiny that, in the economy of nature at large, the addition or subtraction of one mechanical person makes no difference. Imagine the correlation between a tiny, microscopic cell and our own body. The presence or absence of any single cell will have no effect on the life of the body. We cannot be aware of it, and by itself it can have no influence on the life or activity of the human organism. By the same token, a separate individual is far too small to influence the life of the cosmic organism, since it is no more significant to it than one of our cells is to us. This relative obscurity is *precisely* what makes our "evolution" possible.

On an individual basis man serves as an apparatus for development pursuant to the Law of Octaves. Nature made us for a certain purpose—to evolve. We eat not just for ourselves but for an outside purpose, because food cannot evolve by itself without our help. We eat bread, and also take in air and impressions, each of which then develops according to the Law of Octaves. Bread enters as *do,* which contains the possibility and momentum to rise to *re* and *mi* without help. But it cannot become *fa* unless it is mixed with air, which brings energy needed to pass a difficult interval. After that, it needs no help until it reaches *si,* but it then can go no further by itself. Our aim is to help this octave to completion. *Si* is the highest point in ordinary animal life, and is the matter from which a new body can be formed.

Our evolution is the evolution of our consciousness. *And "consciousness" cannot evolve unconsciously.* It is the evolution of our will, and "will" cannot evolve unwillingly. It is the evolution of our power of doing, and "doing" cannot be the result of things that are simply "done."

KNOWLEDGE AND BEING

THERE ARE, SO TO SPEAK, two lines along which our development proceeds: the line of *knowledge* and the line of *being*. Right evolution involves a simultaneous development of both lines that is parallel and reciprocal. In fact, if knowledge gets too far ahead of being, or vice versa, our development goes wrong and sooner or later must come to a standstill.

We understand what "knowledge" means, and we understand the possibility of different levels of knowledge, that it may be lesser or greater, of one quality or another. But we do not understand that the same is true of "being." For us, "being" is synonymous with "existence." We do not understand that there can be different levels of being, that two people who seem superficially identical may have radically different degrees of being, and that a person's knowledge depends on the level of his being. The being of a mineral, a plant and an animal represent different levels of being. And the being of an animal is not the being of a man. But the level of being of two people can actually differ more than the being of a mineral from that of an animal. This is exactly what we do not understand, just as we do not understand that knowledge depends on being. We not only do not understand this but we are actually unwilling to understand it.

In Western culture, we think it is possible for a person to be extremely knowledgeable—for example, a competent scientist who makes discoveries and advances the cause of science—and, at the same time, be, and have the right to be, petty, egotistical, scheming, vain, naive and absent-minded. We take for granted the myth of the "absent-minded professor." Yet this is his being. And we think his knowledge does not depend on his being. We put great value on the level of knowledge, but we care nothing of the level of a person's being, and we have no shame about the low level of our own being. The entire concept is foreign to us, and we cannot comprehend that a person's knowledge depends on the level of his being. In fact, at a given level of being, our potential to acquire knowledge is fixed and limited. Within the bounds of a given level, it is impossible to alter the quality of the knowledge we can acquire. All we can learn is more and more information about the same basic thing. The only way to acquire new kinds of knowledge is to change the nature of our being.

The most characteristic feature of modern man is the *absence of inner unity,* along with a complete lack of those traits we most like to ascribe to ourselves, that is, "lucid consciousness," "free will," an "invariable 'I,'" and the "ability to 'do.'" The dominant aspect of our being, the feature that explains this deficiency and *everything else lacking* in us, is *sleep.* Contemporary man is born, lives and dies asleep. But what *knowledge* can a sleeping person have? If we consider this, bearing in mind that *sleep* is the primary characteristic of our being, it will at once become clear that if we really want knowledge, the first thing we must think about is how to wake up, how to change our *being.*

Maintaining a *balance* between our knowledge and our being is even more important than developing either one separately. This is particularly true in regard to the independent development of knowledge, which is completely undesirable, although it is precisely this *one-sided* development that people often find most attractive. But knowledge without being is theoretical, abstract and irrelevant to life. Developing only the line of knowledge creates someone who knows quite a lot but is unable to do anything, a person who *does not understand* what he knows, who is without *appreciation* and does not distinguish between one kind of knowledge and another. On the other hand, someone who develops only along the line of being and disregards knowledge has the capacity to do a great deal but has no idea what to do or why. This person would do whatever his subjective feelings happen to dictate, which may lead him greatly astray and cause him to commit grave mistakes. In either case, both knowledge and being are brought to a standstill, and neither can develop any further.

In order to understand the nature of knowledge, the nature of being and their relation to one another, we must first understand their relation to "understanding." *Knowledge is one thing, and understanding is another.* Yet people often confuse these two concepts and do not clearly grasp the distinction between them. Knowledge does not, in and of itself, bestow understanding, so that only increasing one's knowledge will not be sufficient to increase one's understanding. Understanding depends upon the relation of knowledge to being. It is the mean or resultant of knowledge and being. Knowledge and being should always remain about equal because if one gets too far ahead of the other, then understanding will turn out to be further removed from both. At the same time, the relation of knowledge to being does not change merely with the growth of knowledge. It changes only when being grows simultaneously in tandem. In other words, understanding grows only if being also develops.

People do not ordinarily make any distinction between understanding and knowledge. We think that greater understanding is a result of greater knowledge. So, we accumulate knowledge, or what we think is knowledge, but we do not accumulate understanding or even concern ourselves about it. Yet many of us have recognized that at different points in our lives, we have understood one and the same idea, the same thought, in totally different ways. It often seems strange that we could have so misunderstood in the past something that, with our current view of things, we now understand perfectly well. At the same time, we realize that, despite this change in our understanding, our knowledge of the given subject remains as before, that is, we knew just as much about it then as we know now. So, what accounts for the difference? It is our being that has changed, and this has inevitably resulted in a corresponding change in our understanding.

In the context of the practical concerns that comprise everyday life, we know perfectly well the difference between mere knowledge and understanding. We recognize that to *know* and to *know how to do* are two different things, and that *knowing how to do* is not given by knowledge alone. But outside the practical sphere, we have no clear grasp of what "understanding" means. Typically, when we realize that we do not understand something, our first instinct is to try *to find a name* for it. As soon as we find a name, we say that we have understood, but to find a name does not mean to understand. Unfortunately, we are usually satisfied with names. A person who knows a lot of names, that is, a lot of words, is considered to understand a great deal—again excepting, of course, in the sphere of practical life where ignorance immediately becomes apparent.

The difference between knowledge and understanding becomes clear when we realize that knowledge may be the function of one center, whereas understanding is the function of three centers. It is possible for the thinking part alone to *know* something about a given phenomenon, but *understanding* appears only when we *feel* the emotional aspect of it and the sensations connected with it. No one can say that he understands the idea of mechanicalness by virtue of merely knowing it intellectually. In order truly to understand our mechanicalness, we must *feel* it with our whole selves. As we are, when we understand nothing, we think that we understand or, at any rate, are able to understand everything. Then, when we begin to understand, we think that we understand nothing. This is because the *taste of understanding* is so unknown that it seems to be a lack of understanding.

AS ABOVE, SO BELOW

K*NOWLEDGE BEGINS WITH the teaching of the cosmoses.* We know
the terms "macrocosm" and "microcosm," basically meaning
large cosmos and small cosmos, large world and small world. The
universe can be regarded as a large cosmos and man as a small cosmos,
analogous to the large one. This conveys the idea of the unity and
similarity of the world and man.

The teaching of two cosmoses can be found in the Kabbalah and
other more ancient systems, but this doctrine is *incomplete* and unsuited
as a basis for anything else. It is merely a fragment split off from another
esoteric teaching of even greater fullness and antiquity that describes
a series of cosmoses or worlds included one within another. Each cosmos is created in the image and likeness of the greatest cosmos, which
itself contains all of the others. "As above, so below," from *The Emerald
Tablet of Hermes Trismegistus,* is an expression that refers to cosmoses.
But it is essential to know that the *full teaching* on cosmoses speaks not
of two, but of seven cosmoses, included one within another—from the
Absolute as the first cosmos. The idea of two analogous cosmoses, accidentally preserved from a great and complete teaching, is so incomplete—the Microcosm and the Macrocosm stand so far apart—that it is
impossible to see or establish any direct analogy between man and the
world.

In the teaching of cosmoses, each cosmos is a living being that lives, breathes, thinks, feels, is born and dies. All cosmoses result from the action of the same forces and laws. But although the same laws pertain everywhere, they manifest in a different way on different planes of the universe, that is, on different levels. This is why the cosmoses are not quite analogous one to another. Owing to the Law of Octaves, there is no complete analogy between them, just as there is no complete analogy between the different notes of the octave.

It is only *three* cosmoses, taken together, that are similar and analogous to any other three. A single cosmos cannot give a complete picture of the manifestation of the laws of the universe. The way that the laws act on each plane, that is, in each cosmos, is determined by the two adjoining cosmoses above and below it. Therefore, in order to know a given cosmos, it is necessary to know the two adjoining cosmoses, the larger one above and the smaller below. Taken together, these two determine the cosmos that lies between them. Three cosmoses together give a complete picture of the manifestation of the laws of the universe.

The relation of one cosmos to another is different from that of one world to another in the astronomical ray of creation. In the ray of creation, we consider worlds in terms of their actual relation but from our point of view: the moon, the earth, the planets, the sun, the Milky Way and so on. Therefore, the quantitative interrelation of the worlds in the ray of creation is not constant. In one case, or on one level, it is greater—for instance, the relation of the Milky Way to our sun. In another case, on another level, it is less—for instance, the relation of the earth to the moon. But the interrelation of the cosmoses is always the same—that is, each cosmos is related to the adjoining cosmos above as *zero to infinity.*

The teaching on cosmoses has immediate relevance to the idea of expanding our consciousness and increasing our capacity for knowledge. In our ordinary state we are conscious of ourselves in *one cosmos,* and we look at all other cosmoses from the point of view of this cosmos. By expanding our consciousness and intensifying our psychic functions, we can enter the sphere of activity of *two other* cosmoses simultaneously, one larger and one smaller. Thus consciousness does not expand only in one direction, that is, toward the higher cosmos, but also downward in the direction of the lower cosmos. By the very act of expanding our consciousness to a higher cosmos, we include the level of a lower cosmos.

This last idea perhaps explains expressions like "The way up is at the same time the way down." This means that if, for example, we begin to sense the life of the planets, or if our consciousness passes to the level of the planetary world, we begin at the same time to sense the life of atoms, or our consciousness simultaneously passes to their level. In this way, the expanding of consciousness proceeds simultaneously in two directions. And cognition of both the larger and the smaller requires a corresponding change in ourselves.

In looking for parallels and analogies between the cosmoses, we may take each cosmos in three relations—in its relation to itself, in its relation to a higher or larger cosmos, and in its relation to a lower or smaller cosmos. When the laws of one cosmos manifest themselves in another cosmos, the result is called a "miracle." This is neither a violation of nor an exception to any laws. It is a phenomenon that occurs according to the laws of another cosmos. Since these laws are unfamiliar and ultimately incomprehensible to us, we see their manifestation as miraculous. At the same time, in order to understand the laws of relativity, it is useful to examine what happens in one cosmos as though looking from another cosmos, that is, from the perspective of the laws of another cosmos. Everything that happens in a given cosmos will take on a completely different appearance and significance when viewed from the perspective of another cosmos. Many new things appear, many others disappear and, in general, everything seems to be different.

Only the idea of cosmoses can provide a firm basis for the laws of relativity, on which real science and philosophy should be based. Indeed, it is possible to say that *science and philosophy, in the true meaning of these terms, begin with the idea of cosmoses.*

LEVELS OF DEVELOPMENT

I N THE STUDY OF ANCIENT KNOWLEDGE, our first step must be to learn a language that will allow us to establish immediately and precisely what we are talking about, from what perspective, and in what regard. This new language contains hardly any new terminology, but permits us to construct our speech according to a new principle—*the principle of relativity*. It introduces the element of relativity into all concepts, which is precisely what is lacking in ordinary language. Once we have mastered this language, with its help we can receive a great deal of knowledge and information that cannot be transmitted by ordinary language, in spite of all its scientific and philosophical terminology.

The primary characteristic of this new language is that all concepts are defined from the point of view of a single idea—the idea of *evolution*. Of course, this is not evolution in the sense of mechanical evolution, because there is no such thing, but the conscious and volitional evolution that alone is possible. Everything in the universe, from solar systems to man, and from man to atom, is always either rising or falling, evolving or degenerating, developing or decaying. Although degeneration proceeds mechanically, evolution and change toward a higher level cannot be mechanical. Even help from outside can be received only insofar as it is valued and accepted. *Nothing evolves mechanically,* and that which cannot evolve consciously has to degenerate.

The new language takes each object being considered in relation to its potential for evolution, including its *place* on the evolutionary ladder.

Thus many of our most common concepts are divided according to the steps of their evolution. For example, let us again take the idea *man*. In this new language, instead of the single word "man," seven designations are used: man number one through man number seven.

Man number seven means a person who has reached the fullest development possible to man and who possesses all the attributes a person can possess, that is, will, consciousness, permanent and unchangeable "I," individuality, immortality and many other properties that are beyond us but that, in our blindness and ignorance, we ascribe to ourselves. Man number six stands very close to man number seven, differing only in that some of his properties have not yet become *permanent*. Man number five, also for us practically unattainable, is a person who has reached *unity*. Man number four represents an intermediate stage, which we will consider below.

Man number one, number two and number three refer to all those who constitute mechanical humanity, that is, all of the humanity that we know and to which we ourselves belong. Every person is born number one, two or three, and all stand on the same level of development. Man number one is someone in whom the center of gravity of his psychic life lies in the moving center. This is the person of the physical body, whose moving and instinctive functions constantly outweigh the emotional and thinking functions, whose life is characterized by primary themes that have their origin in physical sensation. Man number two is someone in whom the center of gravity of his psychic life is in the feeling center, whose emotional functions outweigh all others—the person of feeling, the emotional person. His life is characterized by primary themes originating in the feeling center, so that people and things are defined by whether he likes them or not, whether they are pleasant or unpleasant, whether he loves them or hates them. Man number three is a person in whom the center of gravity is in the thinking center, whose intellectual functions gain the upper hand over the moving, instinctive and emotional functions. His life is characterized by primary themes that originate in theory, and everything he does must be logically correct.

No one, therefore, is born as man number four. On the contrary, having been born on the level of the first three categories, a person reaches this higher level only as a result of efforts of a definite character. Man number four cannot develop as the result of ordinary, accidental influences, like upbringing or education. He is always the product of work in a "school," which we will discuss below. This person already stands on a different level from that of man number one, two and three. He has an *invariable center of gravity* comprised of his ideas, his valuation of the work for consciousness and his relation to the school. In addition, the psychic centers in him have already begun to be balanced so that one center does not predominate over the others; they work toward a common goal. Man number four begins to know himself and to know where he is going.

Man number five has reached unity. His formation has been crystallized and is no longer changeable like man number one, two and three. But it must be noted that man number five can be the result of right work or the result of wrong work. A person can become number five from number four or *without having been man number four.* In the latter case he cannot develop further, cannot become number six or seven.

The division of humanity into seven categories gives the first conception of *relativity* as applied to mankind, and provides a basis for understanding all the inner and outer manifestations of man, all that belongs to and is created by him. For example, we can now speak of knowledge number one, that is, the knowledge of man number one, which is based upon imitation or instinct, learned by heart, crammed or drilled into a person. A true man number one learns everything just like a parrot or a monkey. The knowledge of man number two is merely whatever he happens to like. What this person does not like remains beyond his ken. Nothing is interesting to him unless it is pleasant, or, if he is sick, he will, on the contrary, know only what he dislikes, what he finds repulsive or terrifying, or what fills him with fear and loathing. The knowledge of man number three is based on subjectively logical thinking, on words and literal understanding. This is the knowledge of bookworms and academicians. Men number three, for example, were

the ones who counted how many times each letter of the Arabic alphabet appeared in the Koran of Muhammad, and used this data as the
basis for an entire scriptural interpretation.

The knowledge of man number four is of a very different kind,
not distorted by the predomination of one center. It is knowledge that
comes from man number five, who has already received it from man
number six, who has in turn received it from man number seven. Of
this knowledge, of course, man number four is able to assimilate only
what he can master with his limited capacity. Nevertheless, in comparison with man number one, two and three, he has made great strides in
freeing his knowledge from its earlier subjectivity and in progressing
along the path toward objective knowledge.

The knowledge of man number five is whole and indivisible. This
person now possesses a single "I," as well as the knowledge that this
entails. It is no longer possible for any one "I" to know something inaccessible to the others. What he knows, the whole of him knows—
a knowledge that is closer to objective knowledge. The knowledge of
man number six is everything that a human being is capable of knowing, though it remains somewhat theoretical and can still be lost. The
knowledge of man number seven is entirely his own and cannot be
taken away. This is the *objective* and completely *practical* knowledge of
All, of Everything.

It is exactly the same with being. There is the being of man number
one, that is, the being of someone living by instinct and sensation; the
being of man number two, of a sentimental or emotional person; and
the being of man number three, of the rational or theoretical person.
From this, it is quite clear why knowledge and being are inextricably
intertwined. It is due to the limitations inherent in their being that man
number one, two and three is never able to acquire the knowledge accessible to man number four, five and above. These people can only understand things in their own way and reduce any idea to their own level.

Absolutely everything relating to man can be divided according to
these seven categories. We can thus speak of the art of man number one,
which is imitative, copying, or crudely primitive and sensuous. There is

art number two, which is cloying and sentimental, and art number three, which is more cerebral. And there must be art number four, number five, and so on. In the same way there exists the religion of man number one, man number two and man number three. All known religions and denominations in the world belong to one of these three categories, which are the only ones we know.

SPIRITUAL WAYS

CERTAIN TEACHINGS COMPARE man to a house of four rooms. We live only in one room, the smallest and most meager of them all, and unless someone tells us about it, we never suspect that there are also three other rooms, filled with treasure. As soon as a person learns of this, he immediately starts looking for the keys to them, especially the fourth which is the most important room of all. When a person has found a way into this room, he really becomes the master of his house, for only then does it belong to him, wholly and forever. The fourth room gives man immortality, and all religious teachings strive to show the way into it.

There are a great many ways, some shorter or longer, harder or easier, but all, without exception, lead or strive to lead in one direction, that is, to immortality. The generally known and accepted ways can be divided into three categories:

1. The way of the fakir
2. The way of the monk
3. The way of the yogi

The way of the fakir is that of struggle with the physical body, of work primarily on the first room. This way is long and difficult, with no guarantee of success. The fakir strives to develop power over the body, physical will, by means of tormenting or even torturing the body. The whole of this way consists of various nearly insuperable physical challenges. The fakir either stands motionless in the same position for hours, days, months or years; or sits with outstretched arms on a rock in sun, rain and snow; or tortures himself with fire or by inflicting extreme pain. If he manages not to get sick and die before developing what may be called physical will, this person may thereby attain the fourth room, or the potential to form the fourth body. But his emotional, intellectual and other functions remain undeveloped. He has acquired will but cannot make use of it to gain knowledge or strive for self-perfection. In any event, he is by now probably too old to begin this new work.

The second way is that of the monk, a way of faith, of religious feeling and sacrifice. Only a person with strong religious emotion and strong religious imagination can become a "monk" in the true sense of the word. This way also is very long and difficult. A monk spends years, even decades, on inner struggle, but all his work is concentrated on the second room, that is, on feelings. Subjecting all his other emotions to one emotion, that is, to faith, he develops internal *unity* in himself, control or will over the emotions. In this way he reaches the fourth room, but his physical body and his thinking functions remain undeveloped. In order to be able to make use of the will he has attained, he must develop his body and his capacity to think, which can only be achieved by fresh sacrifices, hardships and renunciations. In effect, *a monk has to become both a yogi and a fakir.* Very few are capable of undertaking this and even fewer capable of seeing it through to the end. Most either die before reaching this point or become monks in outward appearance only.

The third way is that of the yogi—the way of knowledge, the way of mind. This way is chiefly concerned with the third room, striving to enter the fourth by means of knowledge. The yogi hopes to reach the fourth room by developing his mind, but his body and emotions remain undeveloped and, like those who follow the ways of the fakir and the monk, he is unable to make use of what he has attained. He knows everything but can do nothing. In order to acquire the capacity to act, he must first gain mastery over his body and emotions, again setting to work and obtaining results by means of prolonged efforts. In this case, however, he at least has the advantage of understanding his position, of knowing what is needed, what must be done and in which direction to go. But on the way of the yogi, like those who follow the ways of the fakir and the monk, very few acquire the understanding necessary to know where they are going. Most followers succeed simply in one particular achievement and stop there.

The ways also differ in that each implies a different relationship between the follower and his teacher or leader. The follower of the way of the fakir has no teacher in the true sense of the word. The teacher does not teach but simply serves as an example to be imitated by the follower. On the way of the monk, the follower has a teacher, and part of his duty and work consists of absolute faith and submission to the teacher, of *obedience.* But the essence of this way is faith in God, love of God, a constant striving to obey and serve God, although there may be much that is subjective and contradictory in the follower's understanding of the idea of "God" and of "service to God." On the way of the yogi, the follower cannot and should not do anything without a teacher. In the beginning he simultaneously combines the fakir's imitation of the teacher with the monk's faith in the teacher. But, afterward, the follower on the way of the yogi must eventually become his own teacher. He learns the teacher's methods, internalizes them and eventually applies them to himself.

All three ways of the fakir, the monk and the yogi have one thing in common: they all begin with the most difficult step—the renunciation of all worldly things and a complete change of the follower's life. A follower must give up his home, and his family if he has one, renounce all the pleasures, attachments and duties of life, and go out into the desert, or into a monastery or ashram. From the very first day, as the first step on the way, he must die to the world. Only then can he hope to attain anything on one of these ways.

In order to grasp the essence of this teaching, we have to understand that following one of the *ways* is the *only* possible method by which man's hidden potential can be developed. This in turn shows just how difficult and rare this kind of development is. As far as humanity is concerned, the general law demands an existence that never strays beyond the circle of mechanical influences, the existence of the "man-machine." The development of humanity's hidden possibilities is a way *against the general law, against God*. This is why the ways are so difficult and exclusive. Yet although they are narrow and straight, they are the only means by which anything can be attained. From the perspective of everyday life, especially modern life, the ways appear as insignificant, quite imperceptible phenomena that need not exist at all. But these insignificant phenomena represent *everything* that humanity has at its disposal for the development of man's hidden potential. The ways run counter to everyday life. They are based upon other principles and subject to other laws, which is the essence of their power and significance. In an ordinary human life, even one filled with scientific, philosophical, religious or social interests, there is nothing *and there can be nothing* that can provide the possibilities for development contained in the ways. The ways lead, or rather should lead, to immortality, while ordinary human life, even at its best, can lead only to death. The idea represented by the ways cannot be understood unless we recognize that without their help there is no possibility of man's evolution.

Given the current state of our ordinary cultural life, an intelligent person who is seeking knowledge has virtually no hope of attaining his goal. This is because, in the world in which we live, there is nothing along the lines of fakir or yogi schools, and the religions of the West have degenerated to such an extent that there is nothing alive in them. Alternatives like occult movements and naive experiments in spiritualism will get us nowhere. And the situation would indeed be hopeless were it not for the existence of a *fourth method*, which we will call the "Fourth Way."

The Fourth Way does not require a person to give up and renounce all worldly things, but begins at a point much further along the road than the way of the yogi. This means that, before setting out on the Fourth Way, a follower must already be prepared, that is, he must undergo a serious preparation in ordinary life that embraces many different sides. For this, he must be living in conditions that lend themselves to work on the Fourth Way, or at least do not make it impossible. It must be understood that there are both inner and outer conditions that can create insurmountable barriers to the Fourth Way. Moreover, un-like the ways of the fakir, the monk and the yogi, the Fourth Way has no definite form and must, first of all, be *found.*

At the same time, to set out on the Fourth Way is easier than be-ginning one of the other three ways. It is possible to work and follow this way without giving up the normal conditions of life. One can keep one's job, maintain personal relationships and not renounce anything. On the contrary, on the Fourth Way the life situation in which a fol-lower finds himself, or in which, so to speak, the work finds him, is the *best possible situation* for him, at any rate at the beginning, because it is his natural situation. It is, in a sense, *the person himself,* because our life situation makes us what we are. Any situation different from that cre-ated by life would be artificial for us, and such that the work would not touch every side of our being at once. In the natural conditions of life the Fourth Way affects simultaneously every side of man's being. It is work *on the three rooms at once.*

The Fourth Way differs from the other ways in that the principal demand required of the follower is for understanding. One must do nothing that one does not understand, except perhaps as an experiment under the supervision and direction of one's leader. The more a person understands what he is doing, the greater will be the results of his ef-forts. This is one of the fundamental principles of the Fourth Way. The results of work depend on the degree to which efforts are undertaken purposefully and consciously. No "faith" is required; on the contrary, faith of any kind runs counter to the Fourth Way. A follower must sat-isfy himself of the truth of what he is told before he can do anything at all. The method of the Fourth Way consists in doing something in one room and simultaneously doing something corresponding in the two other rooms—that is, while working on the physical body, one works simultaneously on the mind and the emotions; while working on the mind, one works on the body and the emotions; and while working on the emotions, one also works on the mind and the body. This can be done because followers of the Fourth Way apply a certain kind of knowledge that is unavailable to those who follow the ways of the fakir, monk and yogi, a knowledge that allows work in three directions at once. In addition, on the Fourth Way the work of each follower can be individualized so that he does what, and only what, is *necessary for him*. This is possible because the Fourth Way, which is free of definite forms, dispenses with much of the superfluous or merely traditional practices of the other ways. A follower who attains a certain will can apply it because he has acquired control over his mind, body and emotions. He has also saved a great deal of time by simultaneously working on the three sides of his being in parallel.

The Fourth Way is sometimes called *the way of the shrewd, astute man.* The "shrewd man" knows a certain secret that the fakir, monk and yogi do not know. How he learned this secret is not known. Perhaps he found it in some old books, or perhaps he inherited, bought or stole it from someone. It does not matter. The "shrewd man" knows the secret, and with its help outstrips the fakir, monk and yogi. The fakir takes a whole month of intense torture to produce the energy he needs, and the monk spends a week in fasting, prayer and privations. The yogi, who knows considerably more than the other two, takes less time. He knows what he wants, why he needs it and where to get it. He knows, for example, that it is necessary to produce within himself a certain substance, and that it can be produced in one day by certain mental exercises or by concentrating his consciousness. So he focuses his attention on these exercises for an entire day without allowing a single unrelated thought, and he obtains what he needs. In this way, a yogi is able to accomplish in only one day what would take the monk a week and the fakir a month.

But on the Fourth Way knowledge is even more precise and perfect. A person who follows the Fourth Way knows exactly what substances he needs to achieve his aim, as well as various methods for producing them. And he knows that, with the right knowledge, *the same substances can be introduced into the body from outside.* Instead of spending a whole day in exercises like the yogi, a week in prayer like the monk or a month in self-torture like the fakir, he simply prepares and takes in all the necessary substances, and in this way, like taking a pill, he obtains the desired results without wasting time.

V

THE AIM
OF RELIGION

A CONSCIOUS NUCLEUS

I N CONSIDERING THE ORDERLY connectedness of everything in the universe, we need to recognize that there is nothing accidental or unnecessary in nature. Everything has a specific function; everything serves a specific purpose. Organic life is an indispensable link in the chain of worlds which cannot exist without it, just as it cannot exist without them. Organic life transmits various kinds of planetary influences to the earth, and serves to nourish the moon and help it grow. Yet the earth also is growing, not in size but in the sense that it is acquiring greater consciousness, greater receptivity. The planetary influences that were sufficient at one stage of its existence eventually become inadequate. As the earth begins to require finer influences, it has to have a more subtle and sensitive receiving apparatus. Organic life, therefore, has to evolve and adapt in order to meet the needs of the earth and of the other planets. It is the same with the moon. For a while it can be satisfied with the quality of sustenance that is received from organic life, but eventually the time will come when this nourishment is insufficient and the moon will begin to starve. If organic life cannot satisfy the needs of the moon, it is not fulfilling its function. Thus, in order to serve its purpose, organic life must evolve to the level required by the needs of the planets, the earth and the moon.

We must remember that the ray of creation from the Absolute to the moon is like a growing branch of a tree. The tip of this branch, from which sprout new shoots, is the moon. If the moon does not grow, the entire ray of creation will stop growing or be forced to find another path for its development, perhaps by giving off an alternate branch. Since the moon's growth depends on terrestrial organic life, it follows that the ray of creation depends on it as well. If organic life were to disappear or die, then the entire branch, or the part that lies beyond organic life, would immediately wither. The same thing would happen, albeit more slowly, if organic life were arrested in its development, if it stopped evolving or generally failed to fulfill its purpose. This must be remembered. The segment "earth—moon" in the ray of creation has exactly the same potential for development as each separate branch, but this growth is not guaranteed. It depends on the harmonious and right functioning of its own organic structure. If one part stops developing, then all stop.

Everything that can be said about the ray of creation in general or the specific segment "earth—moon" is equally true in regard to organic life on earth. Terrestrial organic life also is a complex structure whose parts are mutually interdependent, and its general growth also is possible only if the "end of the branch" grows. There are some parts that are evolving, and others that serve as sustenance for them. Within the evolving parts there are cells that are evolving and others that serve to sustain them. And in each separate evolving cell there are parts that are evolving and others that serve as sustenance. But always and in everything it must be remembered that evolution is never guaranteed. It is only potential and can stop anywhere and at any moment.

The evolving part of organic life is humanity. Humanity also has an evolving component, although for now we will consider humanity as a whole. If humanity does not evolve, then organic life will stop evolving, and this in its turn will cause the ray of creation to stop growing. As soon as humanity stops evolving, it will cease to fulfill the function for which it was created; it will become useless and could even be destroyed. The end of evolution could thus mean the end of human life.

There are no external signs indicating which period of planetary evolution we are in, or whether the requirements of the moon and the earth are being met by organic life. We cannot know the stage of evolution of humanity, but should keep in mind that the number of possibilities is limited. Nevertheless, in examining human life from a historical perspective, many people would agree that the human race is going in circles. In one century we destroy everything that we created in another, and whatever technological progress we have made in modern times has occurred at the expense of many other things that were perhaps much more important. Generally speaking, we have every reason to believe that humanity has come to a standstill in its development, from which there is a straight path to degeneration and downfall. A standstill occurs when the appearance of any one thing is immediately counterbalanced by its opposite, for example, when freedom from one situation brings slavery to another.

If we recall the Law of Octaves, we see that an ongoing process cannot be redirected at just any moment. It can be changed and set on a new path only at certain "crossroads," which we call "intervals." In between the intervals it cannot be altered. At the same time, if a process passes by an interval and nothing happens, if there is no change, then from this point onward nothing else can be done. The process will continue as it was and develop according to mechanical laws. Even if people foresee that it will inevitably lead to destruction, they will be unable to change anything. Again, the possibility of change exists only at the points called "intervals."

Of course, there are many people who consider that humanity is not developing as it should, and they come up with various theories that they think should completely transform human life. One person invents one theory, another immediately invents a theory that contradicts it, and yet both expect everyone to believe them. Although life naturally takes its own course, we continue believing in theories, always imagining that we have power to effect change. All these theories are, of course, quite fantastic, chiefly because they ignore the subordinate role that humanity and organic life play in the cosmic process. Intellectual theories put man in the center of everything: It all exists for us—the sun, the stars, the moon, the earth. These theories totally overlook man's insignificance—our nothingness, our transient existence. They assert that if a person wants, he has the power to change his whole life, that the human condition can be changed at will. It is the belief in all these different theories, and the imagined power to effect change, that keeps humanity in its current state. Besides, most ideals for the common good and universal equality not only could never be realized, but would even cause disaster if they were. Everything in nature has its purpose, including conditions of social inequality and human suffering. Eliminating all inequality would destroy the possibility of evolution. Abolishing suffering would do away with a whole series of perceptions for which man exists, and prevent the "shock" that alone can change the situation.

The process of humanity's evolution is completely analogous to the process of evolution for individual man. And it begins in the same way—a certain group of elements gradually becomes conscious. This group attracts some elements to itself, subordinates others, and gradually causes the whole organism to serve its aims rather than merely eat, drink and sleep. This is evolution, the only kind that is possible. In humanity as a whole, as in the individual person, everything begins with the formation of a conscious nucleus. All the mechanical forces of life work to prevent this, just as our own mechanical habits and weaknesses work to prevent us from consciously remembering ourselves.

INNER CIRCLES OF HUMANITY

I N THE DEVELOPMENT OF HUMANITY, there are two different processes, which can be called "involutionary" and "evolutionary." An involutionary process begins consciously in the Absolute, but by the time it reaches the next step the process has already become mechanical and, as it develops, becomes more and more mechanical. An evolutionary process, on the other hand, begins only half-consciously, but then becomes more and more conscious as it develops. It is important to establish when evolution begins and whether it is proceeding. Remembering the analogy between humanity and the individual, we should be able to determine whether humanity can be regarded as evolving.

Can we say, for instance, that human life is governed by a group of conscious people? Well, where are they? Who are they? On the contrary, we see the exact opposite: that human life is actually governed by those who are the least conscious. Can we say that the prevailing elements in human life are those that are the best? Nothing of the sort. On the contrary, we encounter everywhere all kinds of vulgarity and stupidity. Can we say that human life is striving toward unity and harmony? Obviously not. All we see are new divisions, new animosities, new misunderstandings. Thus, looking at the actual state of humanity, we find nothing to suggest that evolution is proceeding. If we compare humanity with an individual person, we see that personality is clearly developing at the expense of essence. That which is artificial, unreal and *not our own* is growing at the expense of what is natural, real and *our own*. Along with this, we see a corresponding growth of automatism in a culture that requires automatic behavior. We are undoubtedly losing whatever capacities for independence we once had, turning into automatons, cogs in a machine. There is no way to say where it will all end and where is the way out—or whether there is an end and a way out. Only one thing is certain: that humanity is becoming more and more enslaved every day. Yet this is a voluntary slavery; no chains are necessary. We are growing fond of our slavery, even proud of it. This is the worst thing for a person seeking inner liberation.

As discussed above, evolution of humanity can proceed only through the evolution of a certain group, which will in turn influence the rest of humanity. Can we say that such a group exists? Perhaps, based on certain signs; but even if it does, we have to acknowledge that this group is very small and, at any rate, quite insufficient to influence the rest of humanity. Or, from another perspective, we can say that humanity in its current state is unable to accept the guidance of a conscious group. People who are asleep cannot recognize those who are awake. We cannot know them or how many they are. The only way to find out is to become like them because, as noted before, no one can see above the level of his own being. If there were, say, *two hundred conscious people* who saw a necessary and legitimate need to change the whole of life on the earth, they could do so. At the present time, however, either these people are too few in number or they do not want to do it. Or, perhaps the time has not yet come, or other people are sleeping too soundly.

This brings us to the issue of esotericism. The life of humanity is governed by influences from two different sources: first, planetary influences that act entirely mechanically and are received by both humanity in general and individual people involuntarily and unconsciously; and second, influences that come from inner circles of humanity, of whose existence and significance the vast majority are no more aware than they are of the influences of the planets. The humanity to which we belong, namely, the historic and prehistoric humanity known as civilization, actually constitutes only the *outer circle of humanity*, within which there are several inner circles that we can envision as concentric, one within the other.

The innermost circle, which is called the "esoteric," consists of people who have attained the highest potential of human development, that is, each one possesses the highest degree of individuality, including an indivisible "I," all possible forms of consciousness and knowledge, and a free and independent will. It is not possible for them either to act in a way that contradicts their knowledge or have knowledge that is not expressed in their actions. At the same time, it is not possible for them to disagree or to understand the same thing in different ways. Therefore, everything they do is entirely coordinated among them and serves a common aim, all without any compulsion whatever because it is based upon a common and identical understanding.

The next inner circle is called the "mesoteric" or middle circle, which includes people who possess all the qualities of the esoteric circle except that their cosmic knowledge is more theoretical. Unlike the esoteric circle, these people know and understand many things that they have not expressed in their actions. They know more than they can do. Nevertheless, their understanding is just as precise, and therefore the same, as that of the esoteric circle. Between them there can be no disagreement or misunderstanding. Each has the same knowledge as the rest and all understand it in the same way. But, as noted, when compared with the esoteric circle, their knowledge is somewhat more theoretical.

The third inner circle is called the "exoteric" or outer circle because it is the outermost of the inner part of humanity. Although its members possess much of what has been attained by the esoteric and mesoteric circles, their cosmic knowledge is more philosophical, that is, it is more abstract than that of the mesoteric circle. What the mesoteric circle *calculates*, a member of the exoteric circle *contemplates*. These people may have knowledge that is not expressed in their actions, but it is not possible for them to have differences in knowledge. What one understands, they all understand.

In literature that acknowledges esotericism, humanity is usually divided into two circles, the "exoteric" and the "esoteric," with the former being equated with ordinary human life. In reality, however, the true "exoteric circle" is already something that, as we are, is very far from us and very high. For ordinary man this circle is already "esoteric."

The "outer circle" is the circle of mechanical humanity to which we belong, the only one we know. Its primary characteristic is the lack of common understanding among its members. Everybody understands everything in his own way, each one differently. Thus it is sometimes called the circle of the "confusion of tongues," that is, the circle in which each one speaks his own particular language, where no one understands or even tries to be understood by anyone else. Mutual understanding is impossible outside of exceptional moments or in insignificant matters, and even then only within the limits of the given *being*. If a person becomes *conscious of this general lack of understanding* and wants to understand and to be understood, this means that he has an unconscious tendency toward the inner circle.

The possibility of understanding depends on a person's entering the true exoteric circle where understanding begins. If we picture humanity in the form of four concentric circles, we can imagine four gates on the circumference of the third inner circle, that is, the exoteric circle, through which people of the outer mechanical circle can enter. The four gates correspond to the four ways considered earlier: the way of the fakir for man number one, the way of the monk for man number two, the way of the yogi for man number three, and the Fourth Way for those who cannot proceed by any of the others. The fundamental difference between the ways is that the first three are tied to permanent forms which have existed almost unchanged throughout long periods of history. These three traditional ways are *permanent* ways within the limits of our historical period, with institutions based on religion. Two or three thousand years ago there were also other ways, and those that exist today were much closer to one another. The Fourth Way differs from the ancient and the existing traditional ways in never being fixed or permanent. It has no specific forms or institutions, and appears and disappears according to its own laws that we do not understand.

Esoteric schools may exist in some countries of the East but are difficult to identify because they look just like any other ordinary monastery or temple. Tibetan monasteries are usually built in a form of four concentric courtyards divided by high walls. Indian temples, especially in the south, are built according to the same plan but in the form of squares contained one within the other. Pilgrims usually have access to the first outer courtyard, as do, on exceptional occasions, followers of other religions and Europeans. The second courtyard is restricted to people of a certain caste or those having special permission. The third courtyard is only for associates belonging to the temple, and the fourth is exclusively for Brahmins and priests. This kind of structure, which is, with minor variations, found everywhere, allows esoteric schools to exist without being recognized. Only one out of dozens of monasteries is actually an esoteric school. But how is it to be recognized? If any of us were able to get inside, we would have access merely to the first courtyard. Only students are allowed in the second courtyard, but we would not know this and would be told admission is restricted to a special caste. As regards the third and fourth courtyards, we would not even know that they exist. And we could travel to any temple we like, and encounter the same order. It is impossible for us to distinguish an esoteric from an ordinary monastery or temple unless someone tells us about it.

RELIGION IMPLIES "DOING"

RELIGION IS A RELATIVE CONCEPT that depends on man's being. The religion of one person may not be at all suitable for another. There is the religion of man number one, consisting of rites, external forms, and the pomp and splendor of ceremony or, on the contrary, of a grim, cruel and savage character. There is the religion of man number two, one of faith, love, adoration and inspiration, which often becomes transformed into persecution and oppression of "heathens" and "heretics." There is the religion of man number three, which is a system of intellectual belief, based on logical deduction, reflection and painstaking interpretation. The religions of these three categories are actually the only ones we know. The religion of man number four, number five and higher is of a totally different kind that we cannot know as long as we remain what we are. We can simply recognize that the religion of a person of one level of being is not suitable for a person of another.

If we take Christianity, we can identify the categories more specifically. We can speak of Christianity number one, which is paganism in the guise of Christianity. Christianity number two is an emotional religion that can be either very pure but without force, or, on the contrary, given to the bloodshed and horror of religious wars and the Inquisition. Christianity number three, such as the various forms of Protestantism, is based on dialectic and argument, on theories. Then there is Christianity number four, of which men number one, two and three have no conception whatever. In actual fact, Christianity number one, two or three can be regarded as nothing more than superficial imitation. In reality, only man number four truly strives to be a Christian, and only man number five can actually be a Christian, that is, have the being of a Christian living in accordance with Christ's precepts.

Every real religion created for a definite aim consists of two parts. The first teaches *what* is to be done, and the second teaches *how* to do it. Since the first part tends to become common knowledge, it gradually changes and deviates from the original teaching. The second part, however, is secretly preserved in special schools, enabling followers to rectify what has been distorted and restore that which has been forgotten. Without this second part, there would be no knowledge of real religion, or it would, at most, become incomplete and subjective. The aim of all religions is to find out how to "do," which involves the laws of life. For man there is what is "done," that is, "mechanics," and there is "doing," which is magic. In life everything is moving, either in evolution or involution, either up or down. The movement does not follow a straight line but proceeds simultaneously in a twofold direction, circling around itself and falling toward the nearest center of gravity. This is the law of falling, usually called the law of motion. These universal laws were known in ancient times, as confirmed by historical events that could not have taken place without this knowledge. From the most ancient times people knew how to use and control these laws of Nature. This directing of mechanical laws by man is magic, and includes not only transformation of substances in the desired direction but also resistance or opposition to certain mechanical influences based on the same laws. People who know these universal laws and know how to use them are magicians. Christ, too, was a magician, a man of Knowledge. He was not God, or rather He was God, but on a certain level.

To develop our soul, to fulfill our higher destiny, is the aim of all religions and schools. Each religion has its own special way, but the aim is the same. Let us imagine man as a house with four rooms. The first is our physical body, corresponding to the carriage in the analogy we considered before. The second room is the feeling center, or the horse.

The third is the thinking center, or the driver, and the fourth room is the master. Every religion understands that the master is not here and seeks to find him. But the master can come only when the whole house is furnished, when all the rooms are furnished. Everyone does this in his own way. If a person is not rich, he furnishes each room separately, little by little. But in order to furnish the fourth room, one must first furnish the other three. The ways of the fakir, the monk and the yogi differ according to the order in which the three rooms are furnished, but all must get to the same objective—like reaching "Philadelphia." This is the basic aim of all religions. Each goes by a special route, with special preparation. Man is three persons with different languages, desires, development and upbringing. But all our functions must be coordinated and all our parts developed. After "Philadelphia," the road is one, and all is the same. We may start as a Christian, a Buddhist, a Muslim, but there is only one religion. We may start from one center, but afterward the others must be developed too. After "Philadelphia" there is a master in charge, who thinks for all, arranges everything and sees that things are right.

ESOTERIC CHRISTIANITY

HALF THE PEOPLE IN THE WORLD are Christian, the other half have other religions. In my view, as a sensible man, this makes no difference—the other half are the same. Therefore, we can say that the whole world is Christian, that the difference is only in name. And the world has been Christian not only for our current epoch but for thousands of years. There were Christians long before the advent of Christianity.

Generally speaking, our knowledge of Christianity and the form of Christian worship is very limited. In fact, we know almost nothing about the history and origin of a number of things. For example, what was the source of the church, of the idea of a temple where the faithful gather to attend services and participate in special rites? Most of us never think about this, or we assume that the external forms of the service, such as the rites and the singing of canticles, were invented by the church fathers, or taken partly from Greco-Roman pagan religions and partly from the Hebrews. But none of this is true. The origin of the Christian church, that is, of the Christian temple, is actually much more interesting. To begin with, the form adopted for the church and liturgy in the first centuries of Christianity could not have been borrowed from Greco-Roman cults or from Hebrew religion, because nothing like it existed in either of these traditions. The Jewish synagogue or Holy Temple and the Greek and Roman temples to various gods were something quite different from the Christian church that appeared in the first and second centuries. The Christian church is actually a school, although this has long been forgotten. Imagine a school where the teachers give lectures and perform explanatory demonstrations without even knowing that this is what they are doing, and where the pupils or simply visitors think these lectures and demonstrations are nothing more than ceremonies and rituals. This is the Christian church of our times.

Neither the Christian church nor its form of worship was invented by the church fathers. It was all taken ready-made from Egypt, although not from the historical Egypt that we are familiar with but from one we do not know. This Egypt occupied the same place but existed much earlier. Only small remnants of it have survived in historical times, and these have been so well preserved in secret that we do not even know where to find them. To say that this prehistoric Egypt was Christian many thousands of years before the birth of Christ is to recognize that its religion was based on the same principles and ideas that constitute true Christianity. These were special "schools of repetition" where, on specific days and in some schools perhaps every day, a public recital presented in condensed form the entire course of science that could be learned at the particular school. Sometimes this recital lasted a week or even a month. Thanks to these repetitions, those who attended the course were able to maintain a lasting connection with the school and retain in their memory all they had learned. Sometimes they would travel great distances just to listen to a repetition and when they went away they felt a renewed relation with the school. On certain special days of the year the recitals were particularly complete and performed with particular solemnity, and these days themselves were given a symbolic meaning. It was these "schools of repetition" that served as a model for the Christian church. In fact, the form assumed by the Christian liturgy represents almost entirely the condensed course of the science dealing with the universe and man. All the individual prayers, hymns and responses had their own meaning in this repetition, as did the holidays and religious symbols, although this meaning was forgotten long ago.

In the practice of Christianity, a person has to learn to pray, just as he must learn everything else. Prayer can be productive if one knows how to pray and is able to concentrate in the proper way. But it must be understood that there are various kinds of prayer, which yield different results. When we speak of prayer and how it can be productive, we usually have only one kind in mind—namely, petition, praying *for* something, or we assume that petition can be part of every other kind of prayer. This, of course, is not the case. Most prayers have nothing to do with asking for things. These are ancient prayers, many of which are much older than Christianity. They are, so to speak, *recapitulations*. By repeating them silently or out loud a person endeavors to experience both mentally and emotionally everything contained within them. And it is always possible to make new prayers for oneself. If, for example, a person says, "I wish to be serious," the most important thing is *how he says it*. He can repeat it to himself ten thousand times a day, but if he is thinking about how soon he will be done, and what he will have afterward for dinner, then he is not praying, just kidding himself. The same words, however, can become a prayer if a person recites them in a certain way: When he says "I," he tries at the same time to think of everything he knows about "I." There is no single "I," only a host of petty "I's" that shout and fight with one another. He wants to be one "I"—the master in the allegory of the carriage, horse, and driver. When he says "wish," he thinks what it means to say "I wish." Is he able to wish? He experiences desires and aversions all the time, but they are not his own—"it wishes" or "it does not wish." He therefore strives to oppose these two impulses with his own "I wish" connected with the aims of work on himself, that is, to introduce the third force into the customary combination of the two forces. When he says "to be," the person thinks about what it means "to be," what "being" means. There is the being of mechanical man, with whom everything is "done," and the being of one who can "do." And it is possible "to be" in different ways. What the person praying wants is not simply "to be" in the sense of "to exist," but in the sense of attaining a certain degree of unity in himself. Thus the words "to be" take on new weight and significance. Finally, when he says "serious," the person thinks what it means to be serious about attaining inner freedom. How he responds is very important. If he understands what this means, if he defines it correctly for himself and feels that he truly desires it, then his prayer can be productive in the sense that it can make him stronger in his resolve. He will notice more when he is not serious about his life and will struggle more to overcome this tendency, actually becoming more serious.

In exactly the same way, a person can recite as a prayer the words "I want to remember myself." What does it mean "to remember"? The person must think about memory. He is struck by how little he remembers, how often he forgets what he has decided, what he has seen, what he knows. His whole life would be different if he could remember. Everything bad has come from his inability to remember. When he says "myself"—again he returns to himself. Which "self" does he want to remember? Is it even worth remembering his entire self, and how can he distinguish what aspects he wants to remember? These thoughts can lead to the idea of work for self-knowledge, and how to engage in it more seriously.

In the Christian liturgy there are a great many prayers just like this, where the point is to reflect upon each word. But they lose all meaning when they are repeated or sung mechanically. Take the everyday prayer "Lord, have mercy!" What does it mean? When one recites this prayer, a person is making an appeal to God. He should therefore give some thought to it, asking himself what God is and what he is. He is asking God to have mercy upon him, but for this God first has to be aware of him, to *take notice of him*. But is he worth taking notice of? And if so, what in him is worth anyone's awareness? And who, then, is to be aware of him? The answer is "God himself," and so forth. You see, all these thoughts and many others should occur to a person every time he utters this simple prayer. And then *it is precisely these thoughts that could do for him what he asks God to do*. But what can he hope to accomplish if his praying consists of nothing more than reciting "Lord, have mercy! Lord, have mercy! Lord, have mercy!" over and over again like a parrot? We know full well that it will do him no good at all.

There is something very wrong at the basis of our usual attitude toward religion. We need to understand that, as noted above, religion is "doing." A person does not merely *think* his religion or *feel* it. Unless we *live* our religion to the fullest extent possible, it is not religion—just philosophy, or maybe even fantasy. Whether we like it or not, we show our attitude toward religion by our actions, and *only by our actions.* Therefore, if our actions are opposed to those required by a given religion, we have no right to claim that we belong to that religion. The vast majority of people who call themselves Christians not only fail to obey the precepts of their religion but actually do not even think that they *should* obey them. Christianity forbids murder, and yet one of the dominant features of human progress is our technique of warfare, of killing other people. How can we call ourselves Christians?

No one has the right to call himself a Christian who does not carry out Christ's precepts. We can say that we desire to be a Christian if we try to carry them out. But if we just ignore them, or scoff at them, or make up our own precepts, or simply forget about them, we have no right whatever to call ourselves Christians. War is the most striking example, but the rest of human life is exactly the same. We call ourselves Christians, but we fail to realize that we do not really want to be Christians. And even if we desired it, this would not be enough. In order to be a Christian, it is necessary not only to desire, but *to be able,* to be one.

In order to be a Christian, one must *be,* that is, be master of oneself. If a person is not his own master, he cannot be a Christian. He is simply a machine, an automaton, and a machine cannot be a Christian. Is it possible for an automobile to be Christian? It is simply a machine that functions mechanically, with no capacity to be responsible. To be a Christian means to be responsible. This possibility comes only when a person at least partially ceases to be a machine, when he begins in fact, and not only in words, to desire to be a Christian.

Christianity says that we should love our neighbor, that we should love all people. But this is impossible. At the same time, it is quite true that it is necessary to love. For this, one first must be able. Only then can one love. Unfortunately, over time followers came to adopt the ideal of what is to be done—to love—and lost sight of the precondition: the capacity to "do," the religion that must precede it. Of course, it would be silly for God to demand from man what he cannot give, and it is not like that. Only recently have people forgotten the precondition. And it is only because they have lost the capacity that it is now impossible. Let us each ask ourselves, simply and openly, whether we can love all people. If we have had a cup of coffee, we love. If not, we do not love. How can this be called Christianity?

In the past, not all people were called Christians. Some members of the same family were called Christians, others pre-Christians, still others non-Christians. So, in one and the same family there could be the first, the second and the third. But now all call themselves Christians without justification. A Christian is a person who is able to fulfill the Commandments, who is able to do all that is demanded of a Christian, both with his mind and his essence. A person who, in his mind, wishes to do all that is demanded of a Christian, but can do so only with his mind and not with his essence, is called a pre-Christian. And one who can do nothing, even with his mind, is called a non-Christian.

VI

SEEKING THE WAY

TO AWAKE

T HERE IS A BOOK OF APHORISMS that has never been and probably never will be published. This book says, *"A man may be born, but in order to be born he must first die, and in order to die he must first awake."* Another passage says, *"When a man awakens he can die. When he dies he can be born."* What does this mean?

"To awake," "to die," "to be born" represent three successive stages of a process. In the Gospels there are often references to the possibility of being "born." Several references are made to the necessity of "dying," and many to the necessity of "awakening" or staying awake, as in, "Watch, for ye know not the day and the hour. . . ." But these three possibilities—to awake or not sleep, to die and to be born—are never presented as related concepts, despite the fact that their relationship is the most important thing of all.

Being "born" relates to the first stage of the growth of essence, the beginning of the formation of individuality, and the appearance of a unified and indivisible "I." But in order to be able to realize or even begin to realize this, a person must die in the sense of becoming free from a thousand petty attachments and identifications that keep him where he is. We are attached to everything in life—our imagination, our stupidity and, perhaps more than anything else, our suffering. We must become free from this attachment to things, identification with things, that keeps alive a thousand useless "I's" in us. These "I's" must die in order that a greater "I" may be born. But how? They do not want to die.

This is where the possibility of awakening comes into play, that is, awakening to our nothingness. To awaken means to realize our complete and absolute mechanicalness and helplessness. And it is not sufficient to recognize this intellectually. We need to see it in clear, simple and concrete facts, in our own lives. When we begin to know ourselves a little, we see many things that are bound to horrify us. When we see something that shocks us, our first reaction is to change it, to get rid of it. But however hard we try, no matter how many efforts we make, we always fail and everything stays the same. Here, we realize our impotence, our helplessness, our nothingness. Or again, when we begin to know ourselves, we see that we have nothing that truly belongs to us. We see that everything we have regarded as our own—our views, thoughts, convictions, tastes, habits, even our faults and vices—none of it belongs to us. All of it has been either formed through imitation or borrowed ready-made from somewhere else. In seeing this, we may feel our nothingness. And in feeling our nothingness, we should see ourselves as we really are, not just for a moment but constantly, never forgetting it.

Being continually aware of our nothingness and our helplessness will eventually give us the courage to "die"—not only mentally but in fact—by renouncing forever those aspects of ourselves that are either obstacles or unnecessary for our inner growth. These obstacles are first of all our "false 'I's,'" and then all the fantastic ideas about our "individuality," "will," "consciousness," "capacity to do," as well as our powers, initiative, determination and so on.

But in order to become constantly aware of something, we must first see it, even if only for a moment. All new powers and capacities for realization always come in the same basic way. At first they appear in flashes at rare and short moments, then more often and for longer, and finally, after a great deal of time and effort, they become permanent. The same applies to awakening. It is impossible to fully awaken all at once. We must first begin to awake for short moments, a moment or two every now and then. However, after having made a certain effort, surmounted a certain obstacle and taken a certain irrevocable decision, we must *die all at once and forever.* This would be very difficult or even impossible were it not preceded by a gradual process of awakening.

There are, however, a thousand things that prevent us from waking up, that keep us in the power of our dreams. In order to act consciously to awaken, we have to know the nature of the forces that keep us in a state of sleep. It must be realized that the sleep in which we exist is not like ordinary sleep but is rather a kind of hypnosis, a hypnotic state that is continually maintained and enhanced. One would think that there were forces that derive some use or profit from keeping us in this hypnotic state and preventing us from seeing the truth and understanding our position.

There is an Eastern parable about a wealthy magician who had a great many sheep. He was also very stingy and refused to hire shepherds or pay for a fence around his pasture. So, the sheep often wandered into the forest and fell into ravines. And, above all, they ran away, for they knew that the magician wanted their hides and meat, and this they did not like.

Eventually the magician found a solution: he hypnotized the sheep. First, he made them think that they were immortal and that no harm would come to them when they were skinned; that, on the contrary, it would be very good for them and they would enjoy it. Second, he suggested that he was a "Good Master" who loved his flock so much that he would do anything in the world for them. In the third place, he suggested that if anything were going to happen to them, it would not happen right away, or at least not that day, and so there was no point in thinking about it. Finally, the magician made his sheep think that they were not sheep at all. To some he suggested they were lions or elephants or eagles, to others men, and to others that they were magicians. After this he never had to worry about his sheep again. They never ran away, but waited patiently for the day when the magician would require their hides and meat.

This parable is a good illustration of man's position. If we could really see and understand the horror of our true situation, we would be unable to endure it, even for one second. We would immediately start trying to find a way out and we would quickly succeed, because *there is a way out*. The only reason we do not see it is that we are hypnotized. "To awaken" for man means "to awaken from hypnosis." This is why it is possible but, at the same time, difficult. There is no organic reason for being asleep. We *can wake up*, at least in theory. But in practice it is almost impossible. As soon as we wake up for a moment and open our eyes, all of the forces that caused us to fall asleep become ten times more powerful. We immediately fall back asleep, all the while *dreaming* that we are still waking up or even awake.

In our ordinary sleep it often happens that we want to wake up, but cannot. Sometimes we think that we are awake, but we actually are still asleep, and this may happen several times before we finally awake. In ordinary sleep, however, once we are awake, we are in a different state. This is not the case with hypnotic sleep. There is no sure way to tell whether we have actually woken up, at least at first. We cannot pinch ourselves to make sure that we are not asleep. And if, God forbid, we have heard there is some way to tell whether we are asleep, our fantasy at once transforms it all into a dream.

DISILLUSIONMENT

I N ORDER TO APPROACH the Fourth Way, we should first have a certain preparation, certain luggage. We should already know what is available through ordinary channels about the ideas of esotericism and hidden knowledge, about the potential for man's inner evolution, and so on. These ideas should already be familiar in order for us to be able to speak about them. It is also useful if we have at least some knowledge of science, philosophy and religion, although being tied to religious forms without understanding their essence will get in the way. If we know little, have read and thought little, it is difficult to talk about ideas.

It can be said that there is one general rule for everybody. In order to approach the Fourth Way seriously, we must be *disillusioned*, first with ourselves—that is, with our abilities—and secondly with all of the old ways. We cannot feel what is most valuable in this teaching unless we are disillusioned with our own efforts and the fruitlessness of our search. A scientist should be disillusioned with his science, a religious person with his religion, a philosopher with philosophy and so on. But we must understand what this means. To say, for instance, that a religious person should be disillusioned with religion does not mean that he should have lost his faith. On the contrary, it means being "disillusioned" with the *instruction and methodology only*, having realized that religious instruction is not enough for him and can lead him nowhere. All traditional religious teachings consist of two parts: the visible and the hidden. To be disillusioned with religion means to be disillusioned with the visible, while simultaneously feeling the need to find and know the hidden part. To be disillusioned with science does not mean a loss of interest in the search for knowledge. It means being convinced that the scientific method as commonly understood is not only of limited usefulness but leads often to absurd and self-contradictory theories, and, having become convinced of this, to begin to search for a better method. To be disappointed in philosophy means being convinced that ordinary philosophy is merely—as it is said in the Russian proverb— pouring from one empty glass into another, and recognizing that we do not even know what philosophy means, even though true philosophy also can and should exist.

No matter what we used to do before, no matter what used to interest us, it is only when we have arrived at this state of disillusionment that we are ready to approach the Fourth Way. If we still believe that our old way could lead to something, or if we have not yet tried all of the ways, or if we still think that we will be able to find or do something on our own, it means that we are not ready for this undertaking. This does not, however, mean that the Fourth Way requires us to give up everything we are used to doing. This is entirely unnecessary. On the contrary, it is often even better for a person to continue as in the past. But he must realize that it is only a job, or a habit, or a necessity.

There is not and cannot be any choosing of the people who come in touch with the ways, including the Fourth Way. In other words, nobody selects us. We select ourselves, partly by chance and partly by having a certain hunger. Whoever is without this hunger cannot be helped by chance. And whoever has a very strong hunger can sometimes stumble upon the beginning of a way despite a host of unfavorable circumstances. But besides hunger a person must already have acquired some knowledge that will allow him to discern the way. Let us say, for example, that an educated man, who knows nothing about religion, comes into touch with a potential religious way. He will see and understand nothing, interpreting it as foolishness and superstition, even though, at the same time, he may have a great hunger formulated intellectually. The same thing applies to someone who has never heard of the practices of yoga, of the development of consciousness and so on. If he comes into touch with a yoga way, everything he hears will be meaningless for him, dead. The Fourth Way is even more difficult. In order to discern and rightly value the Fourth Way, we must have thought and felt, and we must already, in effect, have been disillusioned with many things. We may not have actually tried the ways of the fakir, monk and yogi, but we should at least have known about them, considered them and decided that they are not for us. It is not necessary to understand this literally, or to be aware that we have considered and rejected the other ways, but the results of this disillusionment must be in us to help us to recognize the Fourth Way. Otherwise, we can stand right next to it and never see it.

Everything boils down to being ready to sacrifice one's self-centered freedom. We all struggle, consciously and unconsciously, for freedom, or, rather, for what we think is freedom. And this is what, more than anything else, prevents us from attaining real freedom. But a person who is capable of attaining anything at all comes sooner or later to realize that his freedom is an illusion that he must sacrifice. Then we voluntarily accept conditions that we do not determine—unafraid of losing anything because we know that we have nothing to lose. And in this way we acquire everything. Everything that was real in our understanding, in our inclinations, tastes and desires, all comes back to us, along with not only new things that we could not have before, but also a feeling of inner unity and will. But to get to this point, we have to pass through the crucible of acceptance. And if we want real results, we must accept not only externally but internally. This requires a great deal of determination, which in turn requires a profound understanding that there is no other way, that one can do nothing *by oneself,* but that nevertheless something has to be done.

When we finally realize that we cannot and do not wish to live any longer in the way we have been living, when we really see everything that makes up our life and decide to get to work, we must be honest with ourselves in order not to end up in an even worse situation. And there is nothing worse than beginning to work on oneself and then giving up and finding oneself "between two stools"; it would be much better not to begin. And in order not to begin in vain, or risk self-deception, we need to test our determination over and over again. The most important thing is to determine how far we are willing to go, what we are willing to sacrifice. When confronted with this question, the easiest possible answer is "everything." The fact of the matter, however, is that no one can ever sacrifice everything, and this can never be asked of us. We must define exactly what we are willing to sacrifice, and not bargain about it afterward. Otherwise, we will be in the same position as the wolf in the following Armenian fairy tale:

Once upon a time there was a wolf that slaughtered a great many sheep and reduced many people to tears. One day, for some unknown reason, he suddenly felt pangs of conscience and began to repent of his earlier life. So he decided to reform and to slaughter no more sheep. When he had made up his mind, he went to a priest and asked him to perform a service of thanksgiving.

The priest began the service, and the wolf stood there in the church, weeping and praying. The priest went on and on. Since the wolf had slaughtered many of the priest's own sheep, he prayed earnestly for the wolf's reformation.

Suddenly, the wolf happened to look out a window and he saw a herd of sheep being driven home. He began to fidget, but the priest's prayer kept going on and on, as though it would never end. At last the wolf could contain himself no longer and shouted: "Finish it, Father! Or the sheep will all be gone and I'll be left with no supper!"

This fairy tale describes man very well. We are ready to sacrifice everything except today's dinner. We always want to start big. But the fact is that this is impossible. It is beyond us. We must begin with the small things of today.

THE FIRST THRESHOLD

T HE CHIEF DIFFICULTY in understanding the idea of the way is that people usually assume that *the way* begins on the level of ordinary life. This is quite wrong. The way begins on a level much higher than ordinary life. This is what people do not understand. They assume that the beginning of the way is much easier and simpler than it really is.

We live our lives under *the law of accident* and under two kinds of influences governed by accident. The first are influences created *by life itself,* such as race, country, climate, family, education, society, profession, cultural mores and standard of living. Influences of the second kind are created *outside this life,* such as those of the esoteric inner circle that are under different laws, although also on the earth. These influences differ from the first kind by being *conscious* in their origin, that is, they have been created consciously by conscious people for a definite purpose. Influences of this kind are most commonly found in religious systems and teachings, philosophical doctrines, works of art and so on. Although released into life for a definite purpose, they are conscious only in their origin, and once they enter the vortex of human life, they become mixed with influences of the first kind and become unpredictable. As they begin to change and become distorted through transmission and interpretation, these influences blend with influences of the first kind and in the end become no different from the unconscious influences of life itself.

It is quite possible to distinguish influences arising from ordinary life from those that come from outside it, even though enumerating or cataloguing them is impossible. It is necessary to *understand* the principle. In fact, the whole beginning of the way depends precisely upon this understanding, and upon our capacity to discriminate between the two kinds of influences. Of course, the distribution of the influences will vary from person to person. One person may receive more of the second kind from outside life, another less, and a third almost none at all. This is already fate, and nothing can be done about it. Yet, generally speaking, as far as the normal lives of normal people are concerned, these differences are not of great importance. Conditions are more or less the same for everybody or, more correctly, everyone will experience the same difficulties. The challenge lies in learning to distinguish and separate the two kinds of influences. If we do not see or feel their difference, and do not separate the second kind of influence from the first, their action upon us also is not separated, that is, they act in the same way on the same level as the first kind, and thus produce the same results. If, however, in receiving the influences we begin to discriminate between them, and set apart those that are not created in life itself, then discrimination gradually becomes easier, until eventually we no longer confuse them with the ordinary influences of life.

The results of the influences whose source lies outside life collect together within us. We *remember* them together, *feel* them together, so that they begin to form within us a certain whole, a certain concentration. We do not give ourselves a clear account as to how and why this occurs, or, if we do, our explanation is wrong. Yet the point is not the explanation but the fact that these results coalesce within us and form a kind of *magnetic center* that begins to attract kindred influences and in this manner grows. If it receives sufficient nourishment, and if there is no strong resistance from other sides of personality that result from the first kind of influences, the magnetic center begins to change our orientation, determining in which direction to face and even to move. As the magnetic center develops force, we begin to appreciate the possibility of the way and to look for it. The search may take many years. It also may lead to nothing. This depends upon conditions and circumstances, upon the strength of the magnetic center, and also upon the opposing inclinations against this search, which can divert us at the very moment we are about to find the way.

If the magnetic center acts on us and we really seek the way, or at least feel a need for it, we may meet *another person* who knows the way and is connected, directly or through other people, with a center or source of the influences that created the magnetic center. The influence of this person comes through our magnetic center and *at this point* acts on us, free from the law of accident. This is what must be understood. The influence of the person who knows the way is a special, third kind of influence that differs from the first two in being both *conscious* and *direct*. The second kind of influence is conscious in origin but, when intermixed with the first kind, becomes equally subject to the law of accident. Influences of the third kind can never be subject to the law of accident because they and the actions that arise from them exist outside this law. The second kind of influences can appear and act through books, philosophical systems or rituals, but influences of the third kind only proceed directly, that is, by means of oral transmission from one person to another.

The moment the person seeking the way meets one who knows the way is called the *first threshold* or the *first step*. It is here that the *stairway* begins, the passage between "life" and the "way." Only by going up this stairway can we enter the way, and only with the help of a guide can we ascend. We cannot go up by ourselves. The real threshold of the way is where the stairway ends—after the last step, on a level much higher than that of ordinary life. Thus, the way actually begins from a point that is not in life at all, a level that cannot be explained. It has been said that in ascending the stairway, a person is sometimes unsure of everything. We may doubt our own capacity, what we are doing, the knowledge and competence of the guide. At the same time, what we attain is unstable. Even if we ascend fairly high on the stairway, we may still fall at any moment and be forced to start again from the beginning. Nevertheless, when we pass the last step and enter the way, everything changes. First, the guide is understood and doubts are resolved. At the same time, the guide becomes far less necessary. We may even attain a degree of independence and have a good idea of where we are going. Second, it will no longer be so easy to lose the results of our work and find ourselves again at the beginning in ordinary life. Even if we leave the way, we can never return to the point where we started.

This is almost all that can be said generally about the "stairway" and about the "way," because, as noted, there are different ways that vary greatly from each other. For example, on the Fourth Way there are certain conditions that do not apply to the other ways. One such condition is that, in ascending the stairway, in order to reach a higher step we must help another to reach the step we are on. That person, in turn, must put a third person in his place in order to go higher. Thus, the higher we ascend, the more we depend upon those following us; if they stop, we stop. What a person receives he must immediately pass on. Only then can he receive more. Otherwise, he will lose everything he has already been given.

On the Fourth Way there is not *one* leader. Whoever is the elder is the leader. And there are various possibilities in his relation to the esoteric center. He may know exactly where it is, and how to receive its knowledge and help, or he may have no knowledge of the center itself and only know the person from whom he himself received his knowledge. The results of work do not depend on the leader's knowing the exact origin of his knowledge. But very much depends on whether the ideas come *in actual fact* from the esoteric center and whether he understands the distinction between objective and subjective knowledge, that is, between *esoteric* and scientific or philosophical ideas. Generally, we start with knowledge limited to one step higher than our own, and only in proportion to our own development do we begin to see further and recognize the source of what we know. We should never forget that no one can see higher than his own level. This is a law.

"SCHOOLS" ARE IMPERATIVE

WHAT IS NECESSARY to wake someone up? A good shock. However, when we are fast asleep, one shock is not enough. It takes continued shocks over a long period of time. In this case, there must be someone to administer these shocks. If we want to awaken, we must find and hire someone who will keep shocking us for a long time. But who could do that if everyone is asleep? And what if that person also falls asleep?

There is also the possibility to wake oneself up by mechanical means such as an alarm clock. The problem is that we get used to the alarm clock and soon cease to hear it. So, many alarm clocks are necessary, which are changed regularly. We have to surround ourselves with alarm clocks that are constantly going off and preventing us from sleeping. But here again there are problems. Alarm clocks must be set. To set them, we have to remember they are there, and in order to remember, we must wake up often. Even then, we will end up getting used to all these alarm clocks, and after a while only sleep the better. It will therefore be necessary to come up with new ones and switch them constantly. In time, this may help us to awaken. But there is almost no chance of one person doing all the work of inventing, switching and setting the clocks all alone without outside help. It is more likely that if we undertake this we will still fall asleep, and in our dreams we will continue to come up with new alarm clocks, switch them with the old ones and set them, all the while sleeping like a baby. One person can do nothing.

Waking someone up thus requires the combined efforts of several people who work together as a team. If they decide to struggle together against sleep, they will be able to awaken each other. Even if only one of them wakes up, this can be enough because that person can in turn wake up everyone else. They can also work together with alarm clocks. One person will invent one alarm clock, another person will invent a second kind, and then they trade. Working together, they can be a great help to each other. Without this mutual assistance no one can attain anything.

Therefore, if we want to wake up, the first thing is to look for others who also want to awake and work with them. This, however, is easier said than done. Organizing collective work for self-knowledge requires knowledge that an ordinary person cannot possess. An engagement to produce the results we wish requires careful organization and a leader. Without organization and leadership, our efforts will come to nothing. We may torment ourselves all we want, but it will not wake us up. This is the most difficult thing for many of us to understand. By ourselves, and on our own initiative, we may be capable of great efforts and sacrifices, but without the right conditions, these will all be useless.

Work together usually begins in a small group, which is generally connected with a network of similar groups on different levels that, taken together, constitute what may be called a "preparatory school."

Schools of the religious way demand "obedience" before all else, that is, unquestioning submission of the follower, regardless of understanding. Schools of the Fourth Way, on the other hand, demand understanding before anything else. This is because results of efforts on this way are always proportional to understanding. Yet, in order to awake, we must willingly accept conditions that we need. This kind of acceptance is the first thing to be understood, including understanding why acceptance is necessary. Such an attitude is not that easy, because a person beginning self-study is already used to trusting his own decisions, his self-willed approach to searching. We assume that seeing the necessity for change proves that our decisions and approach are correct, and strengthens our trust in them. But work on ourselves can begin only when we start to question our own way of searching.

Questioning our decisions and accepting the conditions of the school presents insuperable difficulties unless we understand that actually we are not sacrificing or losing anything. Although we have up to this point never really made any decisions at all, we are not aware of this. We think that we have free choice, and find it hard to give up the illusion that we are in control of our own lives. Yet work on ourselves cannot proceed until we begin to be free from this illusion. We must realize that *we do not exist,* and therefore have nothing to lose. We must realize our "nothingness" in the full sense of the word. It is this *consciousness of one's nothingness* that alone can conquer the fear of accepting the conditions of a school of the Fourth Way.

We have to recognize that "schools" are imperative because of the complexity of the human organization. No one is able to *keep watch* on the *whole of himself,* on all his different sides. Only school conditions can do this, with methodology and discipline. By ourselves we are too lazy. We do a great deal without the proper intensity, or we do nothing at all, thinking that we are accomplishing something, or we work too hard on something that does not need it and let pass those moments when intensity is required. At the same time, we go easy on ourselves because we are afraid to do anything we don't want to do. No one can ever work hard enough by himself, as we know from experience. No sooner have we set a goal for ourselves than we immediately begin to be indulgent and try to accomplish it as easily as possible. This is not work in the sense of work on oneself. In work on oneself the only effort that counts is *super-effort,* that is, effort which goes beyond what is usual and necessary. Ordinary efforts are not enough.

A "super-effort" means an effort that is beyond what is necessary to accomplish our purpose. Let us say, for example, that I have been walking all day and am exhausted. The weather is awful; it is raining and cold. By the time I get home in the evening, I have walked, say, twenty-five miles. In the house there is supper on the table; it is warm and cozy.

Instead of sitting down to eat, however, I decide to go back out into the rain and walk another couple of miles down the road before returning home. This would be a "super-effort." While I was walking home the first time, it was simply an ordinary effort, which does not count. I was on my way home, cold, hungry and wet, all of which made me walk. In the second case, I walked because I myself decided to do so. Another form of "super-effort" is some kind of work faster than necessary. For example, I am cleaning up or chopping wood. The work ordinarily takes an hour, but I do it in half an hour. That would be a "super-effort." But in actual practice we can never make ourselves perform super-efforts consecutively or for a long time. The only way to do this is by obeying the will of another person, someone who has a specific method in mind and who will not feel sorry for us.

If we were able to work on ourselves, everything would be simple, and we would have no need for school. But we cannot, for reasons that lie deep in our nature. Let us disregard our self-delusion, the lies we tell ourselves, and so on, and consider only the division of the centers. This by itself makes it impossible to work independently on ourselves. We have to understand that the thinking, feeling and moving centers are interconnected and, in a normal person, their activities are always coordinated. This means that a given activity of the thinking center is always coordinated with specific activities of the feeling and moving centers— that a certain kind of thought is *inevitably* coordinated with a certain kind of feeling (or mental state) and with a certain kind of movement (or posture). And one evokes the other; that is, a certain kind of feeling (or mental state) evokes certain movements or postures and certain thoughts, and a certain kind of movement or posture evokes certain emotions or mental states, and so forth. All of these things are coordinated, and none of them can exist without the others.

Let us say, for example, that we decide *to think* in a new way, but without changing the way we feel. If, however, we dislike a particular person, this feeling immediately brings back our old thoughts, which in turn make us forget our decision to think in a new way. Or, let us suppose that we are used to smoking a cigarette while thinking—this is a moving habit. Although we decide to think in a new way, we light a cigarette and go back to thinking in the old way without noticing it. The habitual movement has brought our thoughts right back to where we started. We have to understand, however, that we can never break this coordination by ourselves. The only way is to have another person present who will exert his will and remind us if we forget our aim. All we can do at this stage of our work is obey. We can do nothing by ourselves.

What we need more than anything else is constant supervision and observation, and we cannot observe ourselves *constantly*. We also need to obey definite rules, which requires us both to remember ourselves and to struggle with our habits. No one can do all this by himself. Our ordinary life is arranged far too comfortably for this kind of work. But in school we find ourselves not only in uncomfortable and unfamiliar conditions but also surrounded by other people. This creates tension between us and the others that helps the work on ourselves, and is indispensable in gradually chipping away our sharp edges.

The formal discipline of a school is the only way to work effectively on the moving center. This is important because its malfunctioning, or its independent or automatic functioning, deprives the other centers of the support needed for working in a new way. They involuntarily follow the moving center, so that this kind of work is often possible only by beginning with the moving center, that is, with the body. A body that is lazy, automatic, and full of stupid habits prevents us from doing any kind of real work.

WORK IN GROUPS

ORK FOR SELF-KNOWLEDGE must be organized by a person who understands its challenges and aims, who knows its methods, that is, by someone who has passed through such organized work himself. On the Fourth Way the elder is the leader. In fact, the engagement in groups cannot begin without a leader, but work with a false or incapable leader will produce only negative results.

An important feature of groups is that their composition is not determined by the members. The leader selects people he thinks can be useful to one another in the primary aim of *self-study*, an undertaking that can succeed only in a properly organized group. One person alone cannot see himself, but a group of people dedicated to self-study will help each other, whether they intend to or not. It is human nature to see the failings of others more easily than our own, but on the path of self-study we learn that we ourselves possess all the faults we find in others. We see many things in other people that we do not see in ourselves, but we begin to recognize these features as our own and to realize that the other members of the group are like mirrors in which we see ourselves. But, of course, to see oneself in other people's faults and not merely judge them, one must be on guard and sincere with oneself. We must remember that each of us is divided: a part of us wants to wake up, and the other part, our personality, has no such desire. A group embodies a pact concluded between the "I's" of its members to make a common struggle against their own "false personalities."

When a group is organized, there are both general conditions for all and individual conditions for individual members. One general condition is not to disclose what we hear or learn in the group. In this there is no attempt to keep secrets or to restrict us from exchanging views with our family and friends. The point of this condition is that we *are unable to* transmit correctly what is said in the group, and by giving *wrong ideas* we shut others off from the possibility of approaching or understanding anything in connection with the Fourth Way. The other, and equally important, reason for the restriction is as an exercise to keep silent about things that interest us. We would like to speak about such things to everyone with whom we are accustomed to, as we call it, share our thoughts. This is the most mechanical of all desires, and, in this instance, not speaking is the most difficult abstinence of all. But if we understand or at least follow this rule, it will constitute for us the best possible exercise for self-remembering and the development of will.

Another condition that applies to all members is that they be completely honest with the leader. This also must be clearly and properly understood. We do not realize the extent to which our lives are consumed by lying, whether overtly or by *the suppression of the truth*. We are completely unable to be honest either with ourselves or with other people. We imagine that whether to speak the truth is up to us, and, in fact, do not even understand that to learn to be *honest when it is necessary* is one of the most difficult things in the world. Therefore, we have to learn the real difficulty of being honest, and foremost in our relationship with the leader. If someone intentionally lies to the leader, conceals something from him, or is dishonest with him in any other way, this person's presence in the group becomes completely useless. Being untruthful with the leader is even worse than being impolite or uncivil to him or in his presence.

A third general condition is that we never forget *why we came to the group*—that is, to learn and to work on ourselves for self-knowledge, and to learn and work not as we understand it ourselves but as we are told. If, therefore, once we are in the group, we begin to doubt the leader, to criticize what he does, thinking that we understand better how the group should be conducted, and especially if we show lack of respect for the leader, being impatient, harsh or argumentative, this at once puts an end to any possibility of work for self-knowledge. For no such work is possible unless everyone remembers that he has come to learn, not to teach. As soon as someone begins to distrust the leader, then he and the leader can no longer be of any use to each other. And, in this event, it is better for this person to leave and either try to find another leader or to work without one. Trying to work alone will be a waste of time, but in any case it will do less harm than lying, concealing the truth, or mistrusting and resisting the leader.

Finally, in addition to these basic conditions, it is, of course, presumed that the members of the group must work on themselves for self-knowledge. If we merely come to the group and imagine that we are working, or if we think that just being there is enough, or, as often happens, if we look upon our attendance as a pastime, making friends and so on, then there is no point in our continuing in the group. And the sooner we leave on our own or are asked not to come, the better it will be for everyone.

These basic conditions provide the material for rules that are mandatory for all members of a group. Rules serve two purposes: first, they help everyone avoid things that might get in the way, and second, *they help us to remember ourselves.* Yet it is common that, at the beginning, members find rules onerous and even ask whether it is not possible to do away with one or even all of them. Rules seem to be an unnecessary constraint on our freedom or a tedious formality, and when the leader tries to enforce them, we think that he simply does not like us or is somehow dissatisfied with us.

In reality, rules are the first and foremost *help* that participants get from work in a "school." Obviously the rules are not in place to entertain us, to make us happy or to make things easier for us. They are there for one reason only: to make us behave as *"if we were,"* that is, as if we remembered ourselves and realized how we should treat people outside the work, others in the work and the leader. If we remembered ourselves and understood this, rules would not be necessary for us. But we are not able to do this at the beginning of the work, so that rules are indispensable. Of course, in their action rules can never be easy, pleasant or comfortable, but must be the opposite in order to serve their purpose. Rules are the alarm clocks that wake up the sleeping person. But when the alarm goes off and we open our eyes for a second, our first reaction is to be indignant and demand whether there is not some way to wake up without alarm clocks.

All these conditions are for real groups formed to follow the Fourth Way. In true work for self-knowledge, producing infatuation in people is not allowed. And in properly organized groups, no faith is required. All that is asked for is a little trust, and only for a short while, until a person becomes able to verify what he hears. At first it is difficult to tell whether this work is right, whether the directions received are sound. This is where the theoretical basis of the Fourth Way may prove useful, because a person can judge more easily from the perspective of theory. We know what we know and what we do not know, and we know what can be learned by ordinary means and what cannot. Therefore, if we learn something new that cannot be learned in the ordinary way from books or other conventional sources, this can serve to some extent as an indication that the other side of the Fourth Way, the practical side, may also be right. But this, of course, is merely an indication, and not a guarantee. It is still possible to be mistaken.

VII

A PRACTICAL STUDY

BEGINNING SELF-OBSERVATION

S ELF-OBSERVATION, the chief method of self-study, requires a certain understanding of the functions and characteristics of our human machine. We have to understand the correct divisions of the functions we observe, and be able to define them exactly and at once. And this cannot be simply a verbal classification. It must be an inner definition, by taste, by sensation, in the same way we define all inner experiences.

There are two methods of self-observation. The first is *analysis,* or, more exactly, attempts at analysis, by which one tries to determine the causes of what has been observed. The second method is registering, which involves simply *recording* in one's mind what is observed at the moment. In self-observation, especially at the beginning, attempts at analysis should be avoided at all costs. True analysis will become useful only much further down the road, when one has already come to know everything about the functioning of one's machine and the laws that govern it. As we are, if we try to analyze some internal phenomenon that we have observed, our first questions will inevitably be "What is this? And why is it happening this way and not another way?" Once these questions have been posed, we invariably begin to look for answers to them, and stop observing. It is clear that observation and attempts at analysis cannot proceed at the same time.

But even apart from this, analyzing separate internal phenomena without knowledge of the general laws that govern them is a complete waste of time. We must first accumulate a sufficient quantity of material by means of "recording," that is, registering the results of direct observation of what is taking place at a given moment. Analysis becomes possible only when a certain amount of material has been accumulated, and when, at the same time, laws to a certain extent have been understood.

In undertaking self-observation, we have to begin from the beginning. All our previous experience, the results of our earlier attempts at self-observation, must be set aside. Although it may contain valuable material, it is all based upon wrong divisions of the functions and is itself wrongly divided. It is of no use to us, at least at the beginning of self-study. In time, we will learn how to extract and utilize what is of value in our experience. But from the outset, we must begin self-observation as though we had never done so before, as though we were a complete stranger to ourselves.

Observation must begin with the division of functions. The activity of our human machine can be divided into three clearly defined groups, each of which is controlled by its own center. When we observe ourselves, it is important that we differentiate between the three basic functions, and understand that every phenomenon is related to one or the other of them. It is thus crucial that, as we begin to observe, we understand how the functions differ from one another—that is, what is meant by thinking, feeling and moving activity. And in observing, we must try to determine at once to which group or center the perceived phenomenon belongs.

Some people have a hard time understanding the difference between thinking and feeling; others find it difficult to understand the difference between feeling and sensing. Speaking generally, we can say that the thinking function always operates by way of comparison; that is, that intellectual conclusions are the result of comparison. Feeling and sensing, on the other hand, are not rational functions. They do not compare but simply define a given impression by its aspect—by its being pleasant or unpleasant in one way or another, or by its sensory perception, such as its color, taste or smell. Moreover, sensations can be indifferent—neither pleasant nor unpleasant. In the sensation of "white paper" or "red pencil," there is nothing based solely on color that is inherently agreeable or disagreeable. But feeling functions or emotions are always pleasant or unpleasant; there is no such thing as an indifferent emotion.

The difficulty of distinguishing between the functions is compounded by the fact that the way the centers work varies greatly from person to person. Some of us perceive chiefly through our mind, others through feeling and still others through sensation. It is unfortunately very difficult, if not impossible, for people of different modes of perception to understand each other, because they often use different names for the same thing or the same name for different things. Besides this, there can be combinations of perceptual modes, with one person perceiving the world by way of thinking and sensation, another by thought and feeling, and so on. Each mode of perception necessarily implies a specific way of reacting to external events. The result is, first, that in general we do not understand each other and, second, that we do not understand ourselves. Very often a person believes that his thoughts or his mental perceptions are his feelings, that his feelings are his thoughts or, most common of all, that his sensations are his feelings.

As we learn to study the centers, side by side with their right functioning we shall observe their wrong functioning when one center performs the work of another—for example, when the thinking center attempts to feel or pretend to feel, the feeling center attempts to think, or the moving center attempts to think and feel. The feeling center trying to perform the work of the thinking brings unnecessary nervousness or haste in a situation that, on the contrary, calls for calm judgment and deliberation. The thinking center working in place of the feeling center brings deliberation and insensitivity where what is required is a quick decision based on subtlety and nuance. In such cases, the thinking is simply too slow and cannot understand shades of feeling. In the same way, the mind has no appreciation for sensations, which for it are dead, and is incapable of controlling or even following our movements. Finally, the moving center working in place of the thinking produces, for example, mechanical reading or listening, as when we read or listen to words without understanding their meaning. This usually happens when the attention that should be directing the thinking is occupied with something else, and the moving center attempts to replace it. This kind of substitution easily becomes a habit, because the thinking center tends to become distracted not by useful thought or contemplation, but rather by daydreams and the play of the imagination. Observation of these activities is an important part of self-study.

"Imagination" is a principal source of the wrong work of centers. Although each center has its own form of imagination and daydreaming, as a rule both the moving and the feeling centers tend to use the thinking for this purpose. Since "daydreaming" already suits its own inclinations, the thinking center is more than happy to place itself at their disposal. The centers' inclination to daydream derives partly from the laziness of the thinking, when it avoids work directed toward a definite aim. It also comes from the corresponding tendencies of the feeling and the moving centers to keep alive and re-create experiences, both pleasant and unpleasant, whether real or "imagined." Imagination and daydreaming are instances of the wrong work of the thinking center.

After imagination, the next object of self-observation is habits in general. Every adult person is made up entirely of habits, although most of us are unaware of this. All three centers are full of habits, and we can never know ourselves until we have studied all of them. This is particularly difficult because, in order to see and "record" them, we first have to free ourselves from them, if only for a moment. It is impossible to observe a habit while in its grasp, but all it takes to feel and see a habit is to struggle, no matter how ineffectually, against it. If we want to observe how we walk, we will never succeed so long as we continue walking in the habitual way. But if we understand that our usual way is made up of certain habits—for example, taking steps of a certain length, moving at a certain speed and so on—we can change these by taking bigger or smaller steps, or walking faster or slower, and we will learn to observe and study ourselves in the act of walking. If we want to observe ourselves writing, we have to be aware of how we habitually hold our pen, and then try to hold it in a different way. This is how self-observation becomes possible. In order to observe ourselves, we must try to walk not in our habitual way, to sit in unaccustomed positions, to stand when we are accustomed to sitting and to sit when we are accustomed to standing, and to use our left hand instead of our right hand and vice versa. All this will enable us to observe ourselves, particularly in regard to the habits and associations of the moving center.

In the sphere of the emotions, it is very useful to try to struggle against the habit of immediately venting all our unpleasant emotions. Many of us, for example, find it difficult to keep our feelings about bad weather to ourselves, and find it even more difficult to remain silent when we feel as if someone is violating our sense of justice or fairness. Beyond its usefulness as a method of self-observation, the struggle against expressing unpleasant emotions has another significance. It is one of the few cases where we can actually change ourselves and our habits without in turn creating other undesirable habits. Self-observation and self-study should therefore begin, first and foremost, with the struggle against the *expression of unpleasant emotions.*

FORMATORY THINKING

I N T H E P R A C T I C A L S T U D Y through self-observation, it is important to understand the nature of our so-called "thinking" function, which is, in fact, the mechanical part of the thinking center and the center of gravity of our personality.

Our thinking, feeling and moving centers are in themselves animate brains, and they live like corresponding animals incorporated in one body, with each brain acting as a moving factor. These brains are connected with one another, but their intercommunication depends upon the relative strength of their associations. Only if a stimulus is strong enough in one center can a corresponding association be evoked in another, and then only if the stimulus has a particular velocity or intensity that has already become established in us.

The center of gravity of the personality is not animate, but simply an apparatus for thinking, which is located in the head. The connections between this "formatory apparatus" and the centers are open and direct, and all associations reach it. Every local stimulus in the centers, every association, provokes associations in the apparatus. But the matter of the apparatus is inanimate. The apparatus is simply a machine, just like a letter keyboard that transmits every impact.

The best way to illustrate the formatory apparatus is by analogy. It is a factory office with a secretary. Every incoming paper comes to this person, every client who comes in addresses him, and he replies to everything. The answers given are qualified by the fact that this person himself is only an employee. He does not know anything but has instructions, books, files and dictionaries on the shelves. If he has sources in which to look up some particular information, he does so and replies accordingly. If he hasn't, he does not.

This factory also has four partners or directors who sit in four different rooms, although most of the time they are not there. These directors communicate with the outside world through the secretary. They are connected with his office by telephone. If one of them calls and says something, the secretary has to pass it on. But each of the four directors uses a different code that has been agreed upon. When one of them sends a message to be transmitted, the secretary has to decode it before passing it on. He has in the office a quantity of forms and materials that have accumulated over the years. Depending on the director involved, the secretary consults a book, decodes the message and transmits it.

If the directors want to talk to one another, there is no means of direct communication between them. They are connected by telephone, but this telephone works only in good weather and in conditions of calm and quiet, which seldom occur. Since these conditions are rare, the directors send messages through the central exchange, that is, the secretary's office. Since each one has his own code, it is the secretary's job to decode and recode these messages. The directors communicate with people outside in the same way. Everything that comes in or goes out must be decoded and recoded, then forwarded to its destination. Incoming correspondence for one of the directors is forwarded in the appropriate code. But the secretary often makes mistakes and uses the wrong code. The director receives the message and understands nothing. Thus the decoding and recoding depend on this employee, who has no interest in or concern for the business. As soon as the daily grind is over, he goes home. His decoding skill depends on his education, which varies from person to person. One secretary may be a fool, another a good businessperson. There is an established routine in the office, which the secretary follows. If a certain code is needed, he brings out one or another frequently used form that happens to be handy. For every kind of inquiry there are ready-made labels that are immediately affixed.

This is an approximate picture of the state of affairs in our inner organization. The office is our formatory apparatus, and the secretary represents our education, our mechanical points of view, local clichés, theories and opinions that have been automatically formed in us. The secretary has nothing in common with the centers, and indeed not even with the formatory apparatus. He just works there. Education has nothing to do with the centers. A child is brought up thus: "If someone shakes hands with you, you must always do it like this." It is all purely mechanical—in *this* case, you must do *that*. And once established, so it remains. An adult is the same. If someone steps on our corns, we always react in the same way. Adults are like children, and children are like adults—all of us react. The machine works and will go on working in the same way a thousand years hence.

With time, a great quantity of labels accumulates on the office shelves. The longer a person lives, the more labels there are in the office. It is so arranged that all labels of a similar kind are kept in one file. So when an inquiry comes in, the secretary begins to search for a suitable label. To do this he must take out the file, look through and sort it until he finds the right label. A great deal depends on the tidiness of the secretary and in what state he keeps his files. Some secretaries are methodical, others are not. Some keep labels sorted, others do not. One may put an incoming inquiry in a wrong file, others do not. One finds labels at once, another looks for a long time and mixes them all up while searching. Our so-called thoughts are nothing more than these labels taken out of the file. What we call thoughts are not thinking. We do not think. We have different labels: short, abbreviated, long—but nothing except labels. All this chaos is what we call our thoughts.

At the same time, apart from the formatory apparatus, a person does have thoughts. Every center thinks. These thoughts reach the formatory apparatus in the form of stimuli and are then reconstructed mechanically. And this is so in the best cases, for as a rule some centers have hardly any means of accurately communicating their thoughts to the formatory apparatus. Owing to faulty connections, messages either are not transmitted at all or are distorted. But this does not prove the absence of thought. All centers continually function. There are thoughts and associations, but these do not reach the formatory apparatus, and therefore are not manifested. Neither are they sent in another direction—that is, from the formatory apparatus to the centers—and, for the same reason, they cannot get there from outside.

The centers are themselves the same in everyone. The differences between people lie only in the amount of material the centers contain and in the connections between them. Some have more, others less. A person is born like an empty cupboard or storehouse, but then material begins to accumulate. The machine works alike in everyone and the properties of the centers are the same, but, owing to their nature and the conditions of life, the links or connections between centers differ in degrees of sensitivity. The coarsest and most accessible is the connection between the moving center and the formatory apparatus. This connection is the most "audible," like a large pipe, the quickest to form and to be filled. The second is the connection with the sex center. The third is the connection with the feeling center, and the fourth the connection with the thinking center.

The amount of accumulated material and the degree of sensitivity of these connections stand in this gradation. The first connection with the moving center exists and functions in all people, with associations being received and manifested. And the second connection, the one with the sex center, exists in the majority of people. Consequently, most of us live with just these two centers our whole lives—all our perceptions and manifestations originate in these centers and proceed through them. Those whose feeling center is connected with the formatory apparatus are in the minority, with all their perceptions and manifestations proceeding through it. But there is hardly anyone in whom the connection with the thinking center works.

START WITH SMALL THINGS

S ELF-OBSERVATION AND SELF-STUDY, if rightly conducted, can bring us to realize that something is wrong with our machine and our functions in their ordinary state. We realize that we are asleep and that, precisely because of this, we live and work in a small part of ourselves. The vast majority of our possibilities remain unrealized, the vast majority of our powers undeveloped. We feel that we do not get out of life all that it has to give because of definite functional defects in our machine, which in its state of sleep is unable to receive impressions. The idea of self-study takes on new meaning. We see every function as it is now and as it could or should be, and wonder whether it is even worth studying ourselves as we are now. Self-observation brings us to the realization that we have to change.

And in observing ourselves, we notice that self-observation itself brings about certain changes in our inner processes. We begin to understand that self-observation is an instrument of self-change, a means of awakening. By observing ourselves we throw, as it were, a ray of light onto inner processes that up to now have worked in darkness. Under the influence of this light, the processes themselves begin to change. There are many psychic processes that can take place only in the dark. Even a feeble light of consciousness is enough to completely transform the character of a process, and to make many processes altogether impossible.

Self-observation is only possible after acquiring attention. We must recognize that we have no attention in us, and aim to acquire it. For this we have to start on small things. For example, an aspiring pianist can never learn except little by little. If we wish to play melodies without first practicing, we will never play real music. What we play will be cacophonous and make others suffer. It is the same with living and experiencing psychological ideas: to understand anything, long practice is necessary. We must try to accomplish small things first. If we begin by aiming at big things, we will never achieve anything, and our manifestations will act like cacophonous melodies and cause people to hate us.

In order to do what is difficult, we must first learn to do what is easy, recognizing that there are two kinds of doing—automatic doing and doing according to aim. We must take a small thing that we are unable to do now, and make doing it our aim, our God. We let nothing interfere—our only aim is this. Then, if we succeed in doing this, we will be able to take on a greater task. Today, we have an abnormal appetite to do things that are too big for us. We can never do these things. And this appetite keeps us from doing the small things we could do. We have to destroy this appetite and forget big things. We must make going against a small habit our aim.

In our relations with other people, we have to recognize that to endure the manifestations of others is a big thing, the last thing for us. Only a perfect man or woman can do this. So, we start by making our aim the ability to bear one manifestation of one person that we cannot now endure without reacting. If I "wish"—that is, if I "will"—I "can." Without "willing," I never "can." Will is the most powerful thing in the world. The chief cause of our weakness is our inability to apply our will to all three of our centers simultaneously. With conscious will, everything comes.

We have no energy to fulfill voluntary aims because all our strength, acquired at night during our passive state, is used up in negative manifestations. These are automatic, the opposite of positive, willed manifestations. For those who can remember the aim automatically but have no strength to achieve it, there is an exercise that can help. Sit alone for a period of at least one hour. Make all muscles relax. Allow associations to proceed but do not be absorbed by them. Say to them: "If you will let me do as I wish now, I shall later grant you your wishes." Look on the associations as though they belonged to someone else in order to keep from identifying with them. At the end of an hour take a piece of paper and write your aim on it. Make this paper your God—everything else is nothing. Read it constantly, every day. In this way it becomes truly your own, a part of you, at first intellectually, later actually. To undertake a voluntary aim, and to achieve it, gives magnetism and the ability to "do."

IDENTIFICATION

A FUNDAMENTAL CHARACTERISTIC of our attitude toward ourselves and our surroundings is our constant "identification," our tendency to "meld," with whatever has caught our attention, desire or imagination at a given moment. "Identification" is so pervasive that for purposes of observation it is difficult to separate it from everything else. We are always identifying; the only thing that changes is the object of our identification. We identify with a minor challenge that confronts us while completely forgetting the original goal we had set out to accomplish. We identify with a single thought and forget other thoughts, or with a single emotion or mood and forget our broader emotions and moods. This occurs all the time in work on oneself. We become so identified with individual aims that we fail to see the wood for the trees. Two or three trees closest to us represent the whole forest.

"Identifying" is one of our most insidious foes because it penetrates everywhere and fools us just when we think we are struggling against it. To free oneself from identifying is especially difficult because we naturally become more easily identified with things that interest us most, those to which we give our time, effort and attention. The only way to free oneself from identifying is to be constantly on guard and merciless with oneself, that is, ready to see without fear all the subtle and hidden forms that identifying can assume.

It is necessary to pursue the study of identifying to its very roots in oneself. Part of what makes struggling with it so difficult is that we tend to see it as a positive trait. We call it "enthusiasm," "passion," "inspiration," or whatever, and we think that only in this state can we produce good work of any kind. In reality, of course, this is illusion. In fact, identifying actually prevents us from doing anything the least bit sensible. We would immediately change this positive view if we truly understood what this state means: it makes a person into a thing, a piece of flesh; it deprives him of even the small semblance of a human being that he has. In the East, where people smoke hashish and other drugs, it is not uncommon for a man to become so identified with his pipe that he begins to consider he *is* a pipe himself. This is not a joke, but a fact—in the sense of himself he actually becomes a pipe. This is what identifying is. And for this, hashish or opium is entirely unnecessary. Look at how people are in shops, theaters and restaurants, or how they identify with words when they argue or try to prove something, especially when they do not really know what they are talking about. They become greediness or desires, or they become *words,* until nothing of themselves is left.

Identifying is the chief obstacle to self-remembering because a person who is identified is unable to remember himself. The first step in self-remembering is to *not identify.* But in order to do this, one first has to *stop identifying with oneself,* stop calling oneself "I" all the time. We have to keep in mind that there are two in us. There is *oneself*—that is, "I" in us—and there is *another person,* whom we must struggle with and overcome if we wish to attain anything. So long as we identify or are susceptible to being identified, we are the slave of everything that happens to us. "Freedom" means, first and foremost, freedom from identification.

After general forms of identification, we have to study a particular kind, namely identifying with people, which takes the form of "considering" them, that is, reckoning with them, taking them into account. There are several different kinds of "considering." The most prevalent is considering what others think about us, how they treat us, what kind of attitude they seem to have toward us. We always worry that people do not appreciate us, are not sufficiently nice and polite with us. All this torments us, makes us think and suspect. We waste an enormous amount of energy on supposing or guessing, and develop a distrustful and hostile attitude toward others. Petty concerns like how somebody might have looked at us, what he might have thought or said of us, acquire for us an immense significance. All this considering is merely a form of identification, and is wholly based upon our inner demands, our "requirements." We each inwardly "require" that everyone see what a remarkable person we are and that they constantly express their respect, esteem and admiration for us, for our intellect, cleverness, originality, appearance and all our other qualities. These requirements are in turn based on a completely fanciful notion about ourselves, such as often occurs with people of modest ability or appearance. Writers, actors, musicians, artists and politicians, for instance, are almost without exception sick people. And what are they suffering from? First, from an inflated opinion of themselves, then from requirements, and then from considering, that is, being ready and prepared beforehand to take offense at the slightest lack of understanding or appreciation they perceive in other people.

So far, we have been speaking about "internal considering," that is, identifying with others. The opposite of this is "external considering," which can also serve as a means of fighting against it. External considering is based on an entirely different attitude toward people that involves adapting oneself to their requirements and weaknesses. By considering externally, we do what makes life easier for ourselves and for others. External considering requires both a definite knowledge of people, of their tastes, habits and prejudices, as well as a high degree of self-control. We often *sincerely* desire to tell someone what we really think or feel about him. If we are weak, we give in and justify any unpleasant consequences, saying that we did not want to lie or pretend, that we wanted to be honest. Then we convince ourselves that the whole thing was the other person's fault, that we actually wanted to consider him, even not quarrel and let him have his way. But *the other person* did not want to consider us, which made it impossible to deal with him. This is a common human tendency, to begin with a blessing and end with a curse. We start by deciding not to consider and end up blaming others for not considering us. This is an example of how external considering passes into internal considering. But if we remember ourselves, we will also remember that other people are machines just like us. And we will *enter into their position,* put ourselves in their place, and be more able to understand and feel what others think and feel. If we can do this, our relations will become easier.

Right external considering is an important part of our work. It is not uncommon for people to understand perfectly well the need for external considering in their lives, while at the same time neglecting it in the work with others. We assume that because we are in this work we have a right not to consider. As a matter of fact, the opposite is true. In this work, that is, for a person's successful work, ten times more external considering is necessary than in life. This is because *only by external considering* can we show our valuation and understanding of this work, which in turn determines the results that are obtained.

LYING TO ONESELF

W<small>E OFTEN NAIVELY THINK</small> that we can *do*—a conviction that is the most difficult to get rid of. We do not understand the complexity of our makeup, and do not realize that every effort, even if it yields the desired results, produces thousands of unexpected effects and often unwanted ones as well. Chiefly we forget that we are not starting from scratch with a nice clean, new machine. Behind us are many years of misguided, stupid living, of indulging our weaknesses, shutting our eyes to our own mistakes, striving to avoid all unpleasant truths and constantly lying to ourselves, justifying ourselves, blaming others. All this cannot help affecting our machine. It functions poorly and has had to be artificially modified to adapt to its wrong way of working. These modifications, which may be called "buffers," now act to frustrate all our good intentions.

"Buffers" are like the devices connecting the original railway cars, which lessened the shock when they jarred against each other. Without buffers, the shock of one car striking another would have been unbearable and even dangerous to the passengers on board. Buffers softened the effects of these shocks and made them unnoticeable. The same devices are found within man, created not by nature but by us ourselves, albeit involuntarily. They have developed as a result of the mass of contradictions existing in us—contradictory opinions, feelings, sympathies, words and actions. If we were to feel all the contradictions in our lives, we could not live and act as calmly and complacently as we do. There would be constant friction and unrest. But with the help of "buffers," we can cease to feel the contradictions, avoiding the jarring impact of conflicting views, emotions and words. They make our lives easier. Yet buffers make inner development impossible because they lessen shocks, and it is only shocks that can lead us out of the state we live in—that is, wake us up. They lull us to sleep, providing us with the agreeable reassurance that all is well, there are no contradictions and we can sleep in peace.

Buffers play a significant role in the relation between personality and essence. A very important moment in our work is when we begin to distinguish between our personality and our essence. Our real "I," our individuality, can grow only from our essence. But there are obstacles to this growth contained in personality, which is constantly exerting pressure on essence. In order for inner growth to begin, personality must become passive, and essence must become active. This can happen only if buffers are weakened or removed, because it is by buffers that personality holds essence in subjection.

It is by means of buffers that *we can always be in the right.* They thus help us not to feel our "conscience." In ordinary life this concept is taken too simply—as if we had a conscience. Actually, the concept "conscience" in the sphere of the feeling is what the concept "consciousness" is in the sphere of the mind. And just as we have no consciousness, we also have no conscience. *Consciousness* is a state in which a person *knows all at once* everything that he in general knows, and sees how little he actually knows and how many contradictions there are in his knowledge. *Conscience* is a state in which a person *feels all at once* everything that he in general feels, or can feel. We all have countless contradictory feelings, ranging from a deeply hidden sense of our own nothingness and all kinds of fears to the most ridiculous conceit, arrogance and self-satisfaction. To experience all of this *together* would not only be painful but literally unbearable. If a person were suddenly to feel all of these contradictions simultaneously, suddenly to realize that he loves everything he hates and hates everything he loves, that he lies when he tells the truth and tells the truth when he lies, and if he could feel the shame and horror of it all, this would be to experience the state "conscience." No one can live in this state. Fortunately for our peace of mind and our sleep, this state is very rare, and there is no danger of suddenly waking up, thanks to the buffers developed since early childhood.

Nevertheless, conscience is the fire that alone can forge the unity we seek. Waking up is possible only for those who want it and seek it, for those who are ready to struggle long and persistently in order to attain it. For this, it is necessary to go out to meet all the inner sufferings that come from feeling our own contradictions, from the awakening of conscience. Because we all have a multitude of contradictory "I's," even a momentary awakening of conscience is bound to involve suffering. These moments can become longer if one does not resist or turn away out of fear, but instead accepts and tries to prolong them. Then a certain subtle joy, a foretaste of "clear consciousness," gradually will enter into the experience. When there are no contradictions, conscience does not involve suffering but brings a wholly new kind of joy that we are unable to understand.

The concept "conscience" has nothing in common with the concept "morality," which assumes that we have some power of choice over our actions. Morality is based on buffers. In ordinary life truth has no moral value. We can never keep to a single truth. Our truth changes. If for a time it does not change, this is simply because it is maintained by buffers. In addition, we can never *tell the truth*. Sometimes "it tells" the truth; sometimes "it tells" a lie. Consequently, our sense of what is true and false is worthless because our truth and falsehood depend not on us but on chance, on accident. This is also the case with regard to our words, thoughts and feelings. In order to understand truth and falsehood in life, we must understand falsehood in ourselves, the constant lying to ourselves that goes on all the time.

VIII

A WORK FOR
CONSCIOUSNESS

A DIFFERENT KIND OF
OBSERVATION

THE STARTING POINTS of self-observation are as follows:

1. We are not one.
2. We have no control over ourselves. We do not control our own mechanism.
3. We do not remember ourselves. If a person says, "I am reading a book," and does not know that he is reading, this is one thing. But when he is conscious that "I" is reading, that is self-remembering.

If we observe ourselves in a right way, we will discover a great deal about our being and our existence. In the first place, we will learn incontrovertibly that everything we do, think, feel and say is the result of external influences, and that nothing comes from ourselves. We will see and understand that we are, in fact, nothing more than automatons whose actions are dictated by external stimuli. We will, in short, realize our complete mechanicalness. With us everything gets "done"; we do not "do" anything. We are machines controlled by accidental shocks from outside. Each shock calls one of our "I's" to the surface. A new shock comes along, and this "I" disappears and a different one takes its place. With every change there is a new "I." We will begin to understand that we have no control over ourselves, that we do not know what we may say or do the next moment, that we cannot answer for ourselves even for the shortest length of time. We will also come to realize that if no change occurs in us and we do nothing unexpected, this is simply because nothing has changed outside that acts on us. We will understand that our actions are determined entirely by external influences, and we will realize that there is nothing stable and unchanging in us from which control could come, not a single invariable function or state.

Self-observation brings us to realize that we do not remember ourselves. This "forgetfulness," that is, one's inability to remember oneself, is the most characteristic feature of our being and the cause of everything in us. This shows itself in many ways. We do not remember our decisions, the promises we have made to ourselves, what we said or felt a week, a day, or even an hour ago. We begin work of some kind, but after a while we do not remember *why* we started it in the first place. This is particularly true in the case of work on oneself. We are able to remember our promises to others but only with the help of artificial associations *educated* into us as part of our upbringing, associations that, in turn, are connected with other artificial notions such as "honor," "honesty," "duty" and so on. But, in general, we can say that for every one thing we remember, we forget ten others that are just as important. And we particularly easily forget things about ourselves, especially the mental records of impressions previously registered. We do not remember what we thought or what we said, and we do not remember *how* we thought or *how* we spoke.

To say that one does not *remember oneself* is, most importantly, to recognize that one does not sense or feel *oneself*, one is not conscious of *oneself*. With us, observation "takes place," just as our speaking, thinking or laughing "takes place." We do not sense or feel "I"—that *I* observe, *I* notice, *I* see. Everything "is noticed," "is seen." In order really to observe oneself, one must first of all *remember oneself*. Observations without self-remembering are worthless because we ourselves are not included in our observations. At the same time, self-remembering is difficult, requiring many things besides conscientious effort. In fact, if we work conscientiously, we will remember ourselves not more but less.

It is necessary to observe oneself differently than we do in ordinary life. We need to have a different attitude than before, a different inner posture. We want knowledge—that is, to "know"—but what we have had until now is not "knowing." It is only mechanical collecting of information in which our cognition is not our own but merely the function of what goes on in us. For example, in a lecture one person listens with his mind and another with his feeling. When asked to repeat what is heard, each retells it in his own way in accordance with his inner state at the moment. If an hour later the first person hears something unpleasant and the second is engaged in solving a mathematical problem, the first will repeat what he heard colored by his feeling and the second will do it in a logical form. All this is because only one center is working—in this case, either mind or feeling.

We must learn to listen in a new way. The knowledge we have had up to now is the knowledge of one center—knowledge without understanding. Are there many things we know and at the same time understand? For instance, we say that we know what electricity is, but do we understand it as clearly as we understand that two and two make four? The latter we understand so clearly that no one can prove to us the contrary. But with electricity it is different. Today it is explained to us in one way and we believe it. Tomorrow we will be given a different explanation that we will also believe. Understanding, however, is perception not by one but by at least two centers. There exists a more complete perception, but for the moment it is enough if we make one center monitor the other. If one center perceives and the other approves or rejects the perception, this is understanding. If an argument between centers fails to produce a definite result, it will be half-understanding. Half-understanding is also no good. It is necessary that everything we listen to should be listened to not with one but with at least two centers. Otherwise, it will be, as before, a mere accumulation of new information.

TO SEE THE WHOLE

WHEN WE COME TO REALIZE not only that we need to study ourselves but also to work and ultimately transform ourselves, the character of our self-observation must change. Up to this point we will have studied the details of the work of the centers, trying only to be an impartial witness and register specific phenomena. We will have studied the work of the machine, like the functioning of wheels and levers. Now we must begin to see ourselves, that is, to see not individual details but everything taken as a whole—the whole of ourselves as others see us.

For this we must learn to take "mental photographs" of ourselves at various moments of our lives and in various emotional states. These photos must not be of details but of the whole as we see it, containing simultaneously everything that we can perceive in ourselves at a given moment—emotions, moods, thoughts, sensations, postures, movements, tones of voice, facial expressions and so on. If we succeed in capturing interesting moments, we will in turn collect an entire album of pictures that, taken together, will show us quite clearly what we are. But it is not so easy to take these photos at the most interesting moments, how to catch characteristic postures, facial expressions, emotions and thoughts that express our being. If we succeed in taking enough such photos, we will see that the idea we have always had of ourselves is very far from reality.

Instead of the man or woman we thought we were, we will see

quite another person. This "other" person is oneself and, at the same time, not oneself. It is the version of ourselves as other people know us, as we imagine ourselves and as we appear in our actions and words, but not quite such as we actually are. For, as we all know, there is a great deal that is unreal, invented and artificial in this other person whom other people know. We must learn to divide the real from the invented: in fact, to divide ourselves in our self-observation and self-study. We must realize that we indeed consist of two persons. One is the person we call "I" and whom others call by our given name. The other is the real "I," which appears only for very brief moments and which can become firm and unchanging only after a long period of work for self-knowledge.

So long as we take ourselves as *one person,* we will never change from what we are. Our work on ourselves starts from the moment we begin to feel *two persons* in ourselves. One is passive, and all it can do is observe and register what is happening to it. The other, which calls itself "I," is active and speaks of itself in the first person. But it is, in reality, only the one with the given name. This is the first realization that we can have. Once we begin to feel two persons in ourselves, we will soon see that we are completely in the power of this "other person." No matter what we plan or do or say, it is never "I" that will actually do or say it, but always this other person. And, of course, he will do or say it, not as "I" would have done, but in his own way, with his own personal shade of meaning, which often completely changes what "I" intended.

From this perspective, there is a definite danger that arises from the very beginning of self-observation. Although it is "I" who begins self-observation, the effort is immediately taken over and continued by the "other person," who will from the very first step alter it in a way that may seem incidental but, in fact, transforms it completely. Let us suppose, for example, that we hear the description of this method of self-observation, being told that we must divide ourselves with "I" on one side and the "other person" with a given name on the other side. And we divide ourselves *literally as we hear it.* "This is 'I,'" we say, "and that is the 'other person.'" We never use our own name for the "other person," finding that unpleasant. Moreover, we call "I" the aspects we like in ourselves, or at any rate what we consider to be strong, while we call the "other person" what we do not like or what we consider to be weak. On the basis of this division, we go on to make all sorts of wrong judgments about ourselves, having already fooled ourselves on the most fundamental point—that is, defining the "other person" as a fictional construct instead of an aspect of ourselves as we really are.

We cannot even imagine how unpleasant it is to use our own name in speaking of ourselves in the third person. We try to avoid it in any way we can, calling ourselves an imaginary name that nobody ever has or will use, or simply "he" or "she." In this connection those of us who like to use our first name, last name or nickname when we talk to ourselves are no exception. When it comes to self-observation, we prefer to call ourselves some invented name.

When we understand our utter impotence in the face of our "other person," our attitude toward ourselves ceases to be indifferent. At this point self-observation becomes observation of this other person. We understand that this person is nothing but a mask we wear in a part we play unconsciously and, try as we might, cannot stop playing, a part that makes us do and say thousands of stupid things that we otherwise would never do or say. We feel that we are in the power of this person and, at the same time, that we are not this person. We begin to be afraid of his taking over and changing everything we intend to do, and we regard him as our "enemy." His desires, tastes, sympathies, thoughts, opinions, are either opposed to our own or have nothing in common with them. Yet this person is our master. We are the slave, with no will of our own, no way even to express our desires because he takes control of everything we try to say or do.

On this level of self-observation, we must understand that the whole aim is to free oneself from this "other person." Of course, one cannot in fact be free because this person is oneself. So we must find a way to master him and make him do, not what he wants, but what we ourselves want to do. This "other person" will thus cease to be the master and become the servant. The first stage of work on oneself consists in separating oneself from this person mentally, in actually being separated and remaining apart. But we must bear in mind that the whole attention must be concentrated on this "other person," for one is unable to explain *what one really is*. We can nevertheless explain this person to ourselves and with this we must begin, remembering at the same time that we are not this person.

Self-observation is very difficult. The more one tries, the more one will realize this. For a long time we imagine that we see and know ourselves. And then a point comes when we practice not for results but to understand that we cannot observe ourselves. I am speaking of objective self-observation. Objectively, we are unable to see ourselves for a single minute, because it is a different function, the function of the master. If it seems that we can observe ourselves for five minutes, this is wrong. If for twenty minutes or one minute—this is equally wrong. If we realize simply that we cannot see ourselves, it will be right. To come to this is our aim.

SEPARATE ONESELF
FROM ONESELF

A T OUR BIRTH, three separate machines are born that continue to develop until we die. These are our body, our personality and our essence, which have nothing in common among themselves. Their formation does not depend on us in any way. Their future development, the development of each one separately, depends on the given qualities we possess in ourselves and the conditions that happen to surround us, such as environment, circumstances, geography and so on. For the body, these factors are heredity, geography, food and movement. Personality is formed in the course of our life exclusively through what we hear and read. Essence, which is purely emotional, is the result, initially, of what is received from heredity before the formation of personality, and, later, of the subsequent influence of sensations and feelings with which we live.

The development of all three starts from the first days of life and proceeds independently of one another. Thus it may happen, for instance, that the body begins its life in favorable conditions, on healthy ground, and, as a result, is brave, but this does not necessarily mean that the person's essence is of a similar character. In the same conditions, essence may be weak and cowardly. Its development does not necessarily follow that of the body. A person may be physically strong and healthy, yet as timid as a rabbit.

The center of gravity of the body, its soul, is the moving center. The center of gravity of the personality is the thinking center, and the center of gravity of the essence is the feeling center, which is its soul. Just as a person may have a healthy body and a cowardly essence, so personality may be bold and essence timid. Take, for instance, an educated man of common sense. He knows that hallucinations can occur, and he knows that they are not and cannot be real. So, in his personality, he does not fear them. But his essence is afraid of them. If such a phenomenon appears, his essence cannot help being afraid. Thus the development of one center does not depend on that of another, and one center cannot transfer its results to another.

In certain Eastern teachings the body, emotions and mind are incorporated in the analogy of a rig or team with a carriage, horse, driver and master. The carriage is connected with the horse by shafts, the horse with the driver by reins and the driver with the master by the master's voice. But the driver must be able to hear and understand what the master is saying, and he must know how to drive. The horse must be trained to obey the reins, and be properly harnessed to the carriage. And the carriage must be in good working order.

Work on oneself must begin with the driver, which represents the mind. In order to be able to hear the master's voice, the driver must, first of all, *not be asleep*, that is, he must wake up. Then, it may turn out that the master speaks a language the driver does not understand, in which case the driver must learn this language. But this is not all. While he studies this language, he must also learn to drive the carriage, which in turn involves learning to harness, feed and groom the horse, and to keep the carriage in order. After all, what is the point of learning to understand the master if the driver does not know how to do his job? The master might tell him to go somewhere, but he is unable to move because the horse has not been fed or harnessed and the reins are nowhere to be found. The horse represents our emotions, the carriage the body. The mind must learn to control the emotions, which otherwise will always lead the body like a runaway horse pulling its carriage. This is the order in which work on oneself must proceed.

The first step is to "separate oneself from oneself." Although our mind, our thinking, has nothing in common with our essence, it has the tendency to become identified with essence. To separate oneself from oneself means that the mind should stand apart and be independent of essence. Our weak essence can change at any moment, for it is dependent on many influences: on food, surroundings, the time or weather, and a multitude of other factors. Great power is required to give direction to essence and keep essence to it. (Body and essence are the same devil!) But the mind depends on very few influences and so, with minimal effort, it can be maintained in the desired direction. Even a weak person, having no power over his essence, can give the desired direction to his mind. Each of us has enough strength and can have the capacity and power to act differently. Instead of identifying with essence, instead of being merely a function of essence, our mind is capable of functioning independently. Our thinking can be independent. Every grown-up person can achieve this—everyone who has a serious wish.

I will demonstrate my point by an example. Now, in a calm state, not reacting to anything or anyone, I decide to set myself the task of establishing a good relation with Mr. B. because I need him for my business and can do what I wish only with his help. But I dislike Mr. B. He is a very disagreeable person; he understands nothing; he is a blockhead; he is vile, anything you like. I am so made that these traits affect me. Even if I merely look at him, I become irritated. When he begins to talk nonsense, I am beside myself. I am only a man, so I am weak and cannot persuade myself that I should not be annoyed. I shall go on being annoyed. And if the mind becomes merely a function of essence, I will lose my patience. I will think, or rather "it" will think, from the angle of this annoyance: "To hell with it!"

Yet it is possible to control myself. This depends on the seriousness of my wish to gain the end that Mr. B. can help me attain. If I keep to this purpose, to this desire, I shall be able to do so. No matter how exasperated I may be, I will remember this wish. No matter how furious, how beside myself, I am, in a corner of my mind I shall still remember the task I set myself. Although powerless to curb my impatience, or make me feel this or that toward him, my mind is able to remember my aim. I say to myself: "You need him. Don't get mad. Don't be rude to him." It could even happen that I would curse him, or hit him, but my mind would continue to gnaw at me, reminding me that I should not react this way.

This is precisely what anyone can do who has a serious desire not to identify with his essence. This is what is meant by "separating mind from essence." With a serious adult—a simple, ordinary person without any extraordinary powers, but a grownup—whatever he decides, whatever task he has set himself, that task will always remain in his thought. Even if he cannot achieve it in practice, he will always keep it in mind. Even if he is influenced by other considerations, his mind will not forget the aim he has set himself. He has a duty to perform and, if he is honest, he will strive to achieve it because he is a grownup.

No one can help us in this remembering, in this separation of oneself from oneself. A person must do it for himself. Only then, from the moment we have this separation, can another help us. The only difference between a child and an adult is in the mind. Length of life does not mean maturity. A person may live to be a hundred and yet remain a child. He may grow tall and be a child all the same, if we mean by a "child" one who has no independent logic in his thinking. A person can be called "adult" only from the moment his thought has acquired this quality.

When we speak of change, we are speaking of the necessity of inner change. The work needs nothing external, only inside. Outwardly, a person should play a role in everything. He should be an actor. Otherwise, he does not meet the demands of life. One person likes one thing; another, another thing. If we want to be friends with both and behave only in one way, one of them will not like it—and vice versa. We should behave with each of them as he likes it. Then our life will be easier. But inside it must be different.

As things are now, especially in our times, each of us "considers" in a way that is completely mechanical. We react to everything affecting us from outside. Now we obey orders. She is nice, and I am nice. She is rude, and I am rude. I am as she wants me to be, merely a puppet. But she, too, is a mechanical puppet. She also obeys orders mechanically and does what another one wants. We must stop reacting inside. If someone is rude, we must not react inside. Whoever manages to do this will be freer. It is very difficult.

WORK WITH THREE CENTERS

BEFORE OUR NATURE WAS SPOILED, all four in our analogy—horse, carriage, driver, master—were one. All had a common understanding, and worked together, labored, rested, ate, at the same time. But the understanding and language have been forgotten. Each part has become separate and lives alone, cut off from the rest. Now, at times, it would be necessary for them to work together, but it is impossible. One part wants one thing, another something else.

The point is to reestablish what has been lost, not to acquire anything new. This is the purpose of development. For this we must learn to distinguish essence from personality, and to separate them. When we can do this, we will know what to change and how. Meantime, we have only one possibility—to study. We are weak, we are dependent—we are slaves. It is difficult to break all at once the habits accumulated over years. Later, it will be possible to replace certain habits with others, although these also will be mechanical. Man is always dependent on external influences—only, some influences hinder, others do not.

To begin with, it is necessary to prepare conditions for work. There are many conditions. At present we can only observe and collect material that will be useful for work. We cannot distinguish where our manifestations come from—from essence or from personality. But if we look carefully, we may understand afterward. While we are collecting material, we cannot see that. This is because ordinarily we have only one attention, directed on what we are doing. Our mind does not see our feelings, and vice versa.

Every animal works according to its constitution. One works more, another less, but each works as much as is natural to it. We humans also work, and among us one is more capable, another less. Whoever works like an ox is worthless, and whoever does not work is also worthless. The value of work is not in quantity but in quality.

Every animal, as already said, works according to what it is. One—say, a worm—works completely mechanically. Nothing else can be expected from it because it has only one brain, a mechanical brain. Another animal works and moves solely by feeling—such is the structure of its brain. A third animal perceives movement, which is called work, only through the mind. Nothing else can be demanded from it because it has no other brain. Nothing more can be expected, as nature created it with this kind of brain. Thus the quality of work depends on what brain or brains there are. When we consider different kinds of animals, we find that there are one-brained, two-brained and three-brained animals.

Man is a three-brained animal. But it often happens that he who has three brains must work, say, five times more than he who has two brains. Man is so created that more work is demanded from him than he can produce according to his constitution. It is not man's fault, but the fault of nature. His work will be of value only when he gives to it up to the furthest limits of possibility. Normally the work of man requires the participation of feeling and thought. Working like this means that we feel what we are doing and think why and for what purpose, how we are doing it now, how it had to be done yesterday and how today, how we will have to do it tomorrow, and how it is generally best to get it done, whether there is a better way. If we work rightly, we will succeed in doing better and better work. But when a two-brained creature works, there is no difference between its work yesterday, today and tomorrow.

It is essential to work differently. Each of us must work for himself; others can do nothing in our place. If we can make, say, a cigarette in a right way, we already know how to make a carpet. All the necessary apparatus is given to man for doing everything. Every person can do whatever others can do. If one can, everyone can. Genius, talent, is all nonsense. The secret is simple—to do things as a three-brained being. Whoever can think and do things in a right way can at once do a thing as well as another person who has been doing it wrongly all his life. What has to be learned by this other one in ten years, the newcomer learns in two or three days, and he then does it better than the one who spent his life doing it. I have met people who, before learning, had worked in a wrong way all their lives, but when they had learned, they could easily do work they had never even seen before, the finest as well as the roughest. The secret is very simple and easy—we must learn to work as a three-brained being.

The essence of right work is that the moving, feeling and thinking centers work together to produce an action. There is a thousand times more value even in polishing the floor as it should be done than in writing twenty-five books. But before starting to work with all three centers together, each must be prepared separately to be able to concentrate, remembering that it consists of three parts. The moving center is more or less adapted, although it must be trained to work with the others. The second, as difficulties go, is the thinking center, and the most difficult of all is the feeling center. Although we can already succeed in small things with our moving center, neither the thinking nor the feeling center can concentrate at all. Marshaling thoughts in a desired direction is merely mechanical concentration that is not the goal. It is important to know how to *not depend* on associations.

The chief cause of our wrong way of working is our limited development, the fact that we educate nothing but the mind. We know how to behave with such and such a person: "Good morning. How do you do?" But it is only the driver who knows this. Sitting on his box, he has read about it. But the horse has no education at all. It never went to school. It has not even been taught the alphabet. It knows no language. The horse was also capable of being taught, but we forgot all about it. And so it grew up an abandoned orphan. Only the driver was taught.

He knows languages, knows where such and such a street is. But he cannot drive there alone. If any of us thinks that self-study will help and we will be able to change, we are completely mistaken. Even if we read all the books, study for a hundred years, master all knowledge, all mysteries—nothing will come of it. Because all this knowledge will only belong to the driver. And he, even if he knows, cannot pull the carriage without the horse—it is too heavy.

As for the carriage, its existence was completely forgotten. Yet it is also a part, and an important part, of the team. It has its own life, which is the basis of our life. It has its own psychology. It also thinks, is hungry, has desires, takes part in the common work. It, too, should have been educated, sent to school, but neither the parents nor anyone else cared about it. Originally, our carriage was built for an ordinary town. All the mechanical parts were designed to suit the road, including its many small wheels. The idea was that the unevennesses of the road would distribute the lubricating oil evenly and thus oil the parts. But all this was calculated for a certain town where the roads are not too smooth. Now the town has changed, but the model of the carriage has remained the same. It was made to cart luggage, but now it carries passengers. And it always drives along the same kind of street, the broad boulevards. Some parts got rusty from long disuse. If, at times, the carriage needs to take a different street, it almost always suffers a breakdown and a more or less serious overhaul afterward. After this, it can again run as best it can on the boulevards, but for another street it must first be altered. Every carriage has its own *momentum*, but in a way we could say that our carriage has lost it. And it cannot work without *momentum*.

All of us wish, and can wish, only with one part of ourselves. Again, it is only with the driver, for he has read something, heard something. He has a lot of imagination, and even flies to the moon in his dreams. Those of us who think that we can change ourselves are greatly mistaken. To change something inside is very difficult. Whatever we know, it is the driver who knows it. All our knowledge is just manipulation of the thinking function. Real change is a very difficult thing, more difficult than finding a million dollars in the street.

Inside us we have a horse. It obeys orders from outside. And our mind is too weak to do anything inside. Even if the mind gives the order to stop, nothing will stop inside. What was said about inner change refers only to the necessity of change in the horse. If the horse changes, we can change, even outwardly. If the horse does not change, everything will remain the same, no matter how long we study.

It is easy to decide to change, sitting quietly in our room. But as soon as we meet someone, the horse kicks. The horse inside must change. First of all, we must realize that we are not what we think we are. We are the horse. If we wish to work, we have to begin by teaching the horse a language in which we can talk to it, tell it what we know and show it the necessity of, say, changing its disposition. If we succeed in this, then, with our help, the horse too will begin to learn. But change is possible only inside.

SELF-REMEMBERING

IT IS IMPOSSIBLE TO REMEMBER ONESELF. This is because we want to live by mind alone. Yet the store of attention in the mind (like the electric charge of a battery) is very small. And other parts of us have no wish to remember.

In our analogy of driver, horse and carriage, our mind is the driver. This mind of ours wants to do something, to work differently from the way it worked before. It wants to remember itself. All the interests related to self-change, of self-transformation, belong only to the driver, that is, are only mental. As regards the feeling and body, these parts are not in the least interested in putting self-remembering into practice. The main thing, however, is to bring about a change not in the mind, but in the parts that are not interested. The mind can change quite easily. Yet transformation is not achieved through the mind; if by the mind, it is of no use at all.

Therefore, we must teach, and learn, not by means of the mind but through the feeling and the body. At the same time the feeling and body have neither the language nor the understanding we possess. They understand neither Russian nor English. The horse does not understand the language of the driver, nor the carriage that of the horse. If the driver says in English, "Turn right," nothing will happen. The horse understands the language of the reins and will turn right only to obey the reins. Or, another horse will turn without reins if you rub it in an accustomed place—as, for instance, donkeys in Persia are trained. The same with the carriage—it has its own structure. If the shafts turn right, the rear wheels go left. Then another movement, and the wheels go right. This is because the carriage only understands this kind of movement and reacts to it in its own way. So the driver should know the characteristics and weak sides of the carriage. Only then can he drive in the direction he wishes. But if he merely sits on his box and says in his own language "go right" or "go left," the team will not budge even if he shouts for a year.

We are an exact replica of such a team. Mind alone cannot be called a *man*, just as a driver who sits in a bar cannot be called a driver who fulfills his function. Our mind is like a professional cabby who sits in a bar or at home, and dreams that he is driving passengers to different places. Just as his driving is not a real trip, so trying to work with the mind alone will lead nowhere. We will only become a spinner of theories, a kind of lunatic.

The power of changing oneself lies not in the mind, but in the body and the feeling. Unfortunately, however, our body and our feeling are so constituted that they couldn't care less about anything so long as they are happy. They live only for the present moment, and their memory is short. The mind alone lives for tomorrow. Each part has its own virtue or merit. That of the mind is to look ahead. But it is only the other two that can "do."

Until now, the greater part of our desire and striving has been accidental, arising and existing only in the mind. In our mind there arose accidentally a wish to attain something, to change something. But this existed only in the mind, and nothing has yet changed. There is only this bare idea in the head, and each of us has remained as before. Even if we work ten years with our mind, if we study day and night, remember ourselves in our mind and struggle, we will achieve nothing useful or real. This is because in the mind there is nothing to change. What must change is the disposition of the horse. Desire must be in the horse, and ability, the capacity, in the carriage.

When we say "remember oneself," we mean ourselves. But we ourselves, our "I," are our feeling, our body and our sensation. We ourselves are not our mind, not our thinking. Our mind is merely a small part of us. To be sure, this part has a relation, a connection with ourselves, but only a small relation, so that very little material is allotted to it by our inner organization. If our body and feeling receive for their existence the necessary energy and various elements in the proportion of, say, twenty parts, our mind receives only one part. Our attention is the product of these elements, of this material. Our separate parts each have their own attention; its duration and power are proportionate to the material received. The part that receives more material has more attention.

Since our mind is fed by less material, its attention—that is, its capacity to remember—is short and effective only so long as the material for it lasts. Indeed, if we wish and keep wishing to remember ourselves only with our mind, we shall be unable to remember ourselves longer than this material allows, no matter how much we may dream about it or wish for it, or whatever measures we may take. When this material is spent, our attention vanishes. It is exactly like an accumulator for lighting purposes. It will make a lamp burn so long as it is charged. But when the energy is spent, the lamp cannot give any light even if it is in order and the wiring in good repair. The light of the lamp is our capacity to remember. This should explain why we cannot remember ourselves longer. And indeed we cannot, because this particular capacity is short and will always be short. It is so arranged. It is impossible to install a bigger accumulator or to fill it with a greater amount of energy than it can hold.

Nevertheless, it is possible to increase our self-remembering by bringing in other parts with their own accumulators, and making them participate in the general work. If this is achieved, all our parts will lend a hand and mutually help one another in keeping the desired general light burning. Since we have confidence in our mind, and our mind has come to the conclusion that it is good and necessary for our other parts, we must do all we can to arouse their interest and convince them that the desired achievement is useful and necessary for them too.

We must admit that these other parts—the greater part of our total

"I"—are not in the least interested in self-remembering. More than that, they do not even suspect the existence of this desire in their brother— the mind. We must, therefore, try to have them get to know this wish. If they feel impelled to work in this direction, half the work will have been done. We can begin teaching and helping them. Unfortunately, we cannot at once speak to them in an intelligible way because, owing to their neglected schooling, the horse and the carriage do not know any language fitting for an educated person. Their life and their thinking are instinctive, as in an animal, and so it is impossible to prove to them logically where their future profit lies, or make them see their possibilities. Logic and common sense are not foreign to them, but they received no education. Owing to this, these capacities have degenerated, and their own qualities have become dulled and atrophied. Nevertheless, thanks to their original nature, this condition is not irreversible. It is possible to restore them to their original form by destroying the results, already crystallized, of degenerated habits. Before starting new work, it is necessary to correct old sins.

We wish to remember ourselves as long as possible. But we quickly forget the task we set ourselves because our mind has very few associations connected with it. Other associations engulf those connected with self-remembering. Our associations take place in our formatory apparatus owing to shocks that it receives from the centers. Each shock has associations of its own particular character, whose strength depends on the material that produces them. If the thinking center produces associations of self-remembering, incoming associations of another character, which come from other parts and have nothing to do with self-remembering, absorb these desirable associations. Our problem is to bring our other parts to a point where our thinking center would be able to prolong the state of self-remembering as much as possible, without exhausting the energy immediately.

It should be pointed out that self-remembering, however full and whole, can be of two kinds, conscious or mechanical—remembering oneself consciously or remembering oneself by associations. Mechanical—

that is, associative—self-remembering brings no essential profit but is of tremendous value at the beginning in engaging the participation of all three centers artificially. In the case of our thoughts, this is done through conversations, lectures and so on. For example, if nothing is said, nothing is evoked. We call it "artificial" because we were not born with these thoughts; they are not natural, they do not respond to an organic need. And if thoughts are artificial, then we can create in ourselves for this purpose sensations that are also artificial. The simplest, most accessible sensation can be gotten through uncomfortable postures. We can, for example, assume an unaccustomed position, sitting as we never sat before. For a time it is all right, but after a while we develop an ache. A strange, unaccustomed sensation starts in our legs. We have all the time an urge to shift about, to move our legs in order to change the uncomfortable position. But we have, for the present, undertaken the task to bear it, to keep our whole body in this position, with nothing moving except our head. For the moment we wish to forget about self-remembering, concentrating all our attention, all our thought, on not allowing ourselves automatically, unconsciously, to change our position.

Now, when an unpleasant sensation in the body, especially in certain places, has already resulted, we begin to think in our mind: "I wish. I wish very much to be able often to recollect, in order to remember that it is necessary to remember myself. I wish! You—it is me, it is my body." We say to our body: "You. You—me. You are also me. I wish!" These sensations that our body is now experiencing—and every similar sensation—we wish them to remind us. "I wish to remember. I wish to remember often." All these sensations will remind us.

At a particular moment we come back to our wish to remember ourselves. And we remember by our mind. We ask ourselves, "Do I remember by sensation as well?" As a matter of fact, we find that by sensation we do not remember ourselves. So we assume a particular position and pronounce these words—*"I wish to remember myself."*

When we pronounce the word *"I,"* we have a purely subjective sensation in the head, the chest, the back, according to the state we are in at the moment. We must not say "I" mechanically, as a word, but must note in ourselves its resonance. This means that in saying "I," we must "listen" carefully to the inner sensation and watch, so as never once to say the word "I" automatically, no matter how often we say it.

The second word is *"wish."* In pronouncing it, we sense with our whole body the vibration that occurs in us.

"To remember." Every person, when he remembers, has a barely perceptible process in the middle of the chest.

"Myself." When we say "myself," we mean the whole of ourselves. Usually, when we say the word "myself," we are accustomed to meaning either thought, feeling or body. Now we must take the whole, the atmosphere, the body and all that is in it.

Each of the four elements by itself has its own nature and its own place of resonance. If all four were to resound in one and the same place, it would never be possible for all to resound with equal intensity. Our centers are like accumulators or batteries from which current flows for a certain time if a button is pressed. Then it stops and the button has to be released to enable the battery to refill itself with electricity. But in our centers, which produce a resonance when we pronounce each of the four elements, the expenditure of energy is still quicker than in a battery. They must be given rest in turn, if they are to be able to respond—like bells, each possessing its own battery. While we are saying "I," one bell answers; "wish," another bell; "to remember," a third bell; "myself," the general bell.

It should be noted that each center has its own accumulator of energy. A feature common to us all is that the accumulators of our centers are refilled with energy only insofar as it is being spent, so that no energy remains in them beyond the amount being expended. At the same time, our machine has a general accumulator, independent of the accumulators belonging to the centers. The energy in this general accumulator is generated only when all accumulators work one after another in a certain definite combination. By this means the general accumulator is charged. In this case, the general accumulator becomes an accumulator in the full sense of the word, for reserve energy is collected and stored there during the moments when a certain energy is not being spent.

To prolong the memory of self-remembering is possible by making the energy in us last longer by drawing energy directly from the general accumulator. Although by itself the thinking center can access only its smaller accumulator, a connection with the general accumulator can be effected through the feeling center. Our feeling is much keener and more subtle than our thinking, especially since its formatory apparatus is the only part that works. This explains why so many things are quite inaccessible to the thinking center. If we wish to know and understand more, we must keep in mind that this new knowledge and new understanding will come through feeling. Our aim must be to develop the activity of the feeling center.

IX

TOWARD
LIBERATION

TWO RIVERS

I T WILL BE USEFUL if we compare human life in general to a large
river that arises from various sources and, after a dividing of the waters,
flows in two separate streams. And we can compare the life of any one
person to one of the drops of water composing this river of life.

On account of the unbecoming life of people, it was established by
Great Nature—for the purposes of the common actualizing of everything existing—that, in general, human life on the earth should flow in
two streams, and that individual drops should have the possibility, at
the place where the waters divide, of entering one or the other current.
Thus in the life of humanity there are two directions: active and passive. Laws are the same everywhere. Under the laws, these two currents
continually meet, now crossing each other, now running parallel. But
they never mix. They support each other; they are indispensable to each
other. It was always so, and so it will remain.

The life of all ordinary people taken together can be thought of as
one of these rivers, a river in which each life, whether of a person or
any other living being, is represented by a drop, and the stream in itself
is a link in the cosmic chain. In accordance with general cosmic laws,
the river flows in a fixed direction. All its turns, all its bends, all these
changes have a definite purpose. In this purpose every drop plays a part
insofar as it is part of the river, but the law of the river as a whole does
not extend to the individual drops. The changes of position, movement
and direction of the drops are completely accidental. At one moment a

drop is here, the next moment it is there. Now it is on the surface, now it has gone to the bottom. Accidentally it rises, accidentally it collides with another drop and descends. Now it moves quickly, now slowly. Whether its life is easy or difficult depends on where it happens to be. There is no individual law for it, no personal fate. Only the whole river has a fate, which is common to all the drops. In its current personal sorrow and joy, happiness and suffering—all these are accidental.

But the drop has, in principle, a possibility to escape from this general current and jump across to the other, the neighboring, river. This, too, is a law of Nature. But, for this, the drop must know how to make use of accidental shocks, and of the momentum of the whole river, so as to come to the surface and be closer to the bank at those places where it is easier to jump across. It must choose not only the right place but also the right time, to make use of winds, currents and storms. Then the drop has a chance to rise with the spray and jump across into the other river.

From the moment it gets into the other river, the drop is in a different world, in a different life, and therefore is under different laws. In this second river a law exists for individual drops—the law of alternating progression. A drop comes to the top or goes to the bottom, this time not by accident but by law. On coming to the surface, the drop gradually becomes heavier and sinks. Deep down it loses weight and rises again. To float on the surface is good for it—to be deep down is bad. Much depends here on skill and on effort. In this second river there are different currents, and it is necessary to get into the required current. The drop must float on the surface as long as possible in order to prepare itself, to earn the possibility of passing into a different current, and so on.

But we are in the first river, the passive current of ordinary humanity. As long as we are in it, this river will carry us wherever it may. As long as we are passive, we shall be pushed about and be at the mercy of every accident. We are slaves of these accidents. At the same time, Nature has given us the possibility of escaping from this slavery. Therefore, when we talk about liberation, we are talking precisely about crossing over into the other river, the other current. But, of course, it is not so simple—we cannot cross over merely by wishing it. Strong desire and long preparation are necessary. We have to live through the experience of being identified with all the attractions in the first river. And then we have to die to this river. All religions speak about this death: "Unless we die, we cannot be born again."

This does not mean physical death. From that demise there is no necessity to rise again because if there is a soul, and it is immortal, it can get along without the body, the loss of which we call death. And the reason for rising again is not in order to appear before the Lord God on the day of judgment, as the fathers of the Church teach us. No. Christ and the others spoke of the death that can take place in life, the death of the tyrant from whom our slavery comes, the death that is a necessary condition of the first and principal liberation of man.

If we were deprived of our illusions and all that prevents us from seeing reality—if we were deprived of our interests, our cares, our expectations and hopes—all our strivings would collapse. Everything would become empty and there would remain an empty being, an empty body, only physiologically alive. This would be the death of "I," the death of everything it consisted of, the destruction of everything false collected through ignorance or inexperience. All this would remain in us merely as material, but subject to selection. Then we would be able to choose for ourselves and not have imposed on us what others like. We would have conscious choice.

The question about two rivers refers to essence, as do all real things. The possibility of crossing to the second river depends on desire, strong wish of a very special kind—wishing with essence, not with personality. Our essence is permanent. Our personality is our education, our ideas, our beliefs—things produced by the conditions of our formation. In our essence we have almost nothing, because from the time we were babies we have absorbed almost nothing. So, we must aim to have the possibility to wish, to will, and this can only be attained by a person who realizes his nothingness. We must revalue our values, and this must be based on a real need. One cannot do this revaluation by oneself alone.

Each of us must decide: Is the Way necessary for me or not? If we can be sincere, these values really can change. Even preparation of the mind gives results. But there is a risk. Although our mind changes every day, our essence stays as it is. Occasionally, we may feel with our essence something that is very bad for us, or at least for our peace of mind. We will already have tasted something which, though we forget it, may return. If the impression is very strong, our associations will keep reminding us, and if it is intense, we will be half in one place and half in another. And we will never be quite comfortable. This is good only if a person has a real possibility of change, and the chance of changing.

People can be very unhappy—neither fish nor flesh nor herring. This is a serious risk. Before we think of changing our seat, we would be wise to consider very carefully and take a good look at both kinds of chairs. Happy is the person who sits in his ordinary chair. A thousand times happier is the person who sits in the chair of the angels, but miserable is the one who has no chair. Each of us must decide—is it worthwhile? Now our conscience is relative, but when we change our values, we will have to stop lying to ourselves. When we have seen one thing, it is much easier to see another, and it is more difficult to shut our eyes. We must either stop looking or be willing to take risks.

VOLUNTARY SUFFERING

T HE ANALOGY OF the horse-drawn carriage includes three connections between the four components—the "driver's understanding" that unites him to the master; the "reins" that connect him with
the horse; and the "shafts" and the "harness" that connect the horse
with the carriage. If something is lacking in one of the connections, the
organization cannot act as a unified whole. The connections are therefore just as important as the actual "bodies" represented by the carriage,
horse, driver, and master. Work on ourselves must entail simultaneous
work on both the "bodies" and the "connections," although these are
different kinds of work. The bodies and connections can be illustrated
as follows:

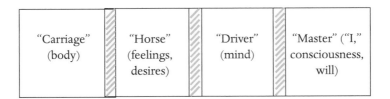

| "Carriage" (body) | | "Horse" (feelings, desires) | | "Driver" (mind) | | "Master" ("I," consciousness, will) |

It sometimes happens that the bodies are developed and functioning, but that the "connections" are not working. In this case, what use
is the whole organization? As with a person whose bodies are undeveloped, the whole organization will inevitably end up controlled *from
below*, that is, not by the will of the master, but by accident. As noted

above, however, work on the bodies—the driver, the horse and the carriage—is one thing, while work on the "connections" is entirely another
matter.

   When a person has only a physical body, it is active and everything
else is passive. In a person with two bodies, the second body functions
actively in relation to the physical body, which allows the consciousness
of the "astral body" to control the physical body. In a person with three
bodies, the third or "mental body" functions actively in relation to the
"astral body" and the physical body, which allows the consciousness of
the "mental body" to control both the "astral body" and the physical
body. In a person with four bodies, the active body is the fourth, which
means that the consciousness of the fourth body has complete control
over the "mental," the "astral" and the physical bodies. The relationships in the case of one body and then of several bodies can be illustrated by symbols for plus (+) as active and minus (−) as passive in the
accompanying diagrams.

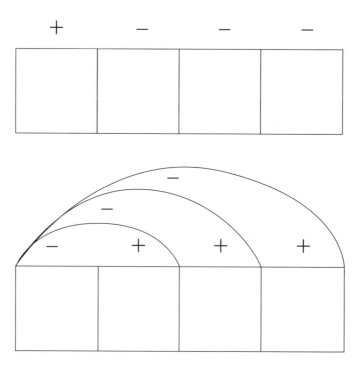

As we can see, these four structures are quite different, depending on the bodies involved. Yet the same order of relationship is possible among the functions in a person with only a physical body. The physical functions may control feeling, thought and consciousness; feeling may control the physical functions; thought may control the physical functions and feeling; or *consciousness* may control the physical functions, feeling and thought.

The possibility of inner change depends upon the horse. So, we should begin to teach the horse a new language, prepare it for the desire to change. The horse and the driver are connected by the reins. At times the driver cannot give orders to the horse because our "reins," which are not made of leather, have the capacity now to thicken, now to become thinner. When they become thinner, the driver cannot control the horse. The same situation exists between the horse and the carriage, that is, the connection of the "shafts."

We have something like magnetism in us, consisting of not only one but several substances formed when the machine is working. When the machine works mechanically, a first substance is produced. When we work subconsciously, another kind of substance is produced. And when we work consciously, a third kind of substance is produced. In terms of the connections between our centers, the first substance corresponds to the "shafts," the second to the "reins," and the third to the substance that permits the driver to hear the passenger, remembering that sound cannot travel in a vacuum.

The master of the carriage is "I," if we have an "I." If we have not, there is always a casual passenger sitting in the carriage and giving orders to the driver. Between the passenger and the driver there is a substance that allows the driver to hear. Whether these substances are here depends on many accidental things. If the necessary substance has accumulated, the passenger can give orders to the driver. But the driver may not be able to order the horse, and so on. Sometimes we can, at others we cannot. It depends on the amount of substance there is. Tomorrow we can, today we cannot. This substance is the result of many things.

One of these substances is formed when we suffer. Here again, the

Law of Three operates. Between the positive and the negative principles there must be friction, suffering. It is suffering that leads to the
third principle. When we are passive, suffering and results happen outside and not inside us. This is a hundred times easier, but inner result is
achieved only when everything takes place inside us. This law is everywhere and in everything, including, for instance, in conversation. When
people talk, one person affirms, another denies. If they do not argue,
nothing comes of these affirmations and negations. If they argue, a new
result is produced, that is, a new conception unlike those of the person
who affirmed or of the one who denied. So, we cannot say our former
conversations never brought any results. There has been a result, but it
has not been for us, only for something or someone outside us. If we
wish to have results in us, we need to bring this law within ourselves,
for ourselves. In order to achieve this, we have merely to change the
field of action of this law. What we have done so far when we affirmed,
denied and argued with others, we need to do within ourselves, so that
the results we get may be subjective.

Only confrontation may produce a result. Whenever there is an
active element, there is a passive element. If we believe in God, we
also believe in the devil. All this has no value. Whether we are good or
bad—it is not worth anything. Only confrontation between two sides
has value. At every moment there may be a conflict in us, but we never
see ourselves. When we begin to look into ourselves, then we will see.
If we try to do something we do not want to do, we will suffer. If we
want to do something and do not do it, we also suffer. There are different kinds of suffering. For instance, we want to tell something but feel it
is best to say nothing. One side wants to speak, the other wants to keep
silent. The struggle produces a substance that collects in a certain place.
Only when much is accumulated can something new manifest itself.

But unconscious suffering brings no results, as, for instance, when
we have no money to buy bread and suffer from hunger. If we have
some bread and do not eat it, this is better. At the same time, if we
suffer with one center, either thinking or feeling, we will go crazy, to a

lunatic asylum. Suffering must be harmonious, with a correspondence between the fine and the coarse.

Every person dislikes suffering. Every person wants to be quiet, choosing what is easiest, least disturbing, and trying not to think too much. Sometimes we are active, at other times we are passive. For one hour we are active, for another hour passive. When we are active we are being spent. When we are passive we rest. But when everything is inside us, we cannot rest. The law acts always. And we suffer whenever we are not mechanically quiet.

In the two rivers, suffering depends on the position of each drop, which at one moment is on the surface, at another moment on the bottom. In the first river, suffering is completely useless because it is accidental and unconscious. In the second river, however, suffering can be voluntary and the law of redemption operates. Today the drop suffers because yesterday it did not suffer enough. The drop can also suffer in advance. Sooner or later everything is paid for. Instead of suffering simply because one feels unhappy, one may suffer for yesterday and to prepare for tomorrow. Only voluntary suffering has value.

THE FIRST LIBERATION

LIBERATION LEADS TO LIBERATION. These are the first words of truth—not truth in quotation marks but truth in the real meaning of the word. This is truth that is not merely theoretical, not simply a word, but truth that can be realized in practice. We need to understand the meaning behind these words.

By liberation is meant the liberation that is the aim of all schools, all religions, at all times. This liberation can indeed be very great. All desire it and strive after it. But it cannot be attained without the first liberation, a lesser liberation. The great liberation is liberation from influences outside us. The lesser liberation is liberation from influences within us.

Inner influences and inner slavery come from many varied sources and independent factors—independent in that sometimes it is one thing and sometimes another, for we have many enemies. There are so many that life would not be long enough to struggle with each of them directly and free ourselves from each one separately. So we must find a method, a line of work, that will enable us simultaneously to destroy the greatest possible number of enemies within us from which these influences come. We have to deal with them indirectly in order to free ourselves from several at the same time.

The chief and most active enemies are vanity and self-love. One teaching even calls them representatives and messengers of the devil himself. For some reason they are also called Mrs. Vanity and Mr. Self-

Love. These representatives of the devil stand unceasingly at the threshold that separates us from the outside, and prevent not only good but also bad external influences from entering. Thus they have a good side as well as a bad side. For a person who wishes to discriminate among the influences he receives, it is an advantage to have these watchmen. But if he wishes all influences to enter, no matter what they may be—for it is impossible to select only the good ones—he must liberate himself as much as possible, and finally altogether, from these watchmen, whom some consider undesirable.

There are many methods and a great number of means to liberate oneself. Personally I would advise trying to free ourselves without unnecessary theorizing simply by active reasoning with ourselves. Through active reasoning this is possible. But if anyone does not succeed, if he fails to do so by this method, there is no other way to go further.

Take, for instance, self-love, which occupies almost half of our time and our lives. If someone, or something, has wounded our self-love from outside, then, not only at that moment but for a long time afterward, its momentum closes all the doors and therefore shuts out life. If I live only inside myself, it is not life. But everybody lives like this.

For instance, let us imagine that I am in a meeting with two people, whom we shall call M. and K. We live together. M. called me a fool—I am offended. K. gave me a scornful look—I am offended. I consider. I am hurt and shall not calm down and come to myself for a long time.

All people are affected like this. We have similar experiences all the time. One experience subsides, but no sooner has it subsided than another of the same nature starts. Our machine is so arranged that there are not separate places where different things can be experienced simultaneously. We have only one place for our psychic experiences. So if this place is occupied with experiences like these, there can be no question of our having the experiences we desire. And if certain attainments or liberations are supposed to bring us to certain experiences, they will not do so if things remain as they are.

Nevertheless, it is when I am connected with the outer world that

I live. And when I examine myself, I connect myself with the outside. So I engage in a different, more active reasoning. M. called me a fool. Why should I be offended? Such things do not hurt me, so I do not take offense. This is not because I have no self-love. Maybe I have more self-love than anyone else. Maybe it is this very self-love that does not let me be offended.

I think, I reason, in a way exactly the reverse of the usual way. He called me a fool. Must he necessarily be wise? He himself may be a fool or a lunatic. One cannot demand wisdom from a child. I cannot expect wisdom from him. His reasoning was foolish. Either someone has said something to him about me, or he has formed his own foolish opinion that I am a fool. So much the worse for him. I know that I am not a fool, so it does not offend me. If a fool has called me a fool, I am not affected inside. But if in a given instance I was a fool and am called a fool, I am not hurt, because my task is not to be a fool. I assume this to be everyone's aim. So he reminds me, helps me to realize that I am a fool and acted foolishly. I shall think about it and perhaps not act foolishly next time. So, in either case, I am not hurt.

K. gave me a scornful look. It does not offend me. On the contrary, I feel sorry for him because of the dirty look he gave me. For a dirty look must have a reason behind it. Can he have such a reason? I know myself. I can judge from my knowledge of myself. Possibly someone had told him something that made him form a bad opinion of me. I am sorry for him because he is so much a slave that he looks at me through other people's eyes. This proves that he is not a concern for me. He is a slave and so he cannot hurt me.

I say all this as an example of reasoning. Actually, the secret and the cause of all such things lies in the fact that we do not know what we are and thus do not possess genuine self-love. In fact, self-love is a great thing. Although self-love, as we generally understand it, is reprehensible, true self-love is desirable and necessary. True self-love—which, unfortunately, we do not possess—is a sign of a high valuation of oneself. If a person has this self-love, it proves what he is.

As said earlier, self-love is a representative of the devil. It is our chief enemy, the main brake to our aspirations and our achievements. It is the principal weapon of the representative of hell. At the same time, self-love is an attribute of the soul. By self-love one can discern the spirit. Self-love indicates and proves that a given person is a particle of heaven. Self-love is I—I is God. Therefore, it is desirable to have self-love.

Self-love is hell, and self-love is heaven. These two, bearing the same name, are outwardly alike but totally different and opposite to one another in essence. But if we look superficially, we can go on looking throughout our whole life without ever distinguishing the one from the other. To distinguish these two is very difficult when we look at others, and still more so when we look at ourselves.

There exists a saying: "He who has self-love is halfway to freedom." Yet among us everyone is full to overflowing with self-love. And in spite of the fact that we are full to the brim with self-love, we have not yet attained one tiny bit of freedom. Our aim must be to have self-love. If we have self-love, by this very fact we shall become free of many enemies in us. We can even become free of these principal ones—Mr. Self-Love and Mrs. Vanity.

Active reasoning is learned by practice. It should be practiced long and in many varied ways.

FREEDOM FROM INFLUENCES

I N ORDINARY MAN everything is governed by the physical body which, in its turn, is governed by external influences. Man is subject to many influences, which can be divided into two categories. First, those that result from chemical and physical causes, and second, those that are associative in origin and are a result of our conditioning.

"Chemico-physical" influences are material in nature and result from the mixture of two substances that produce something new. They arise independently of us and act from without. For example, someone's emanations may combine with our own—the mixture produces something new. And this is true not only of external emanations. The same thing also happens inside a person. Thus we feel at ease or ill at ease when someone is sitting close to us. When there is no accord, we feel ill at ease. Each person has different kinds of emanations, with their own laws, allowing various combinations. Within us emanations of one center form various combinations with emanations of another center. This kind of combination is chemical. Emanations vary, even depending on whether we had tea or coffee.

In considering chemico-physical influences in our different centers, we return to the analogy of the carriage, the horse and the driver, as well as the shafts, the reins and the substance, or "ether," connecting the passenger to the driver. Everything has its emanations and its atmosphere. The nature of each atmosphere is different because each has a different origin, different properties and a different content. They are similar to one another but the vibrations of their matter differ. The carriage, our body, has an atmosphere with its own special properties. Our feelings also produce an atmosphere, the emanations of which may go a long way. When we think as a result of associations, this produces emanations of a third kind. When there is a passenger instead of an empty place in the carriage, emanations are also different, distinct from the emanations of the driver. The passenger is not a country bumpkin; he thinks of philosophy and not about whisky.

"Associative" influences are quite different. If we see a particular form or if someone acts in a certain way, the resulting action on me is mechanical. It touches off some memory or association that gives rise to other associations, and so on. Owing to this shock our feelings and thoughts change. Such a process is not chemical but mechanical. Let us take first the associative influences of "form." Form influences us. If we are accustomed to see a particular form, we are afraid when it is absent. Form gives the initial shock to our associations. Beauty, for example, is also form. In reality, we cannot see form as it is. We only see an image. A second category of associative influence is our feelings—our sympathies or antipathies. Another person's feelings affect us and our feelings react correspondingly. Or sometimes it happens the other way around. It depends on the combinations. Either the other person influences us or we influence him. This influence may be called "relationship." A third kind of associative influence may be called "persuasion" or "suggestion." For example, a person persuades another with words. One persuades us, we persuade another. Everybody persuades, everybody suggests.

These chemico-physical and associative influences come from things that are near to us. But there are also other influences that come from big things, from the earth, from the planets and from the sun, where laws of a different order operate. The earth and the other planets are in constant motion, each with a different velocity. Sometimes they approach one another, at other times they recede from one another. Their mutual interaction is thus intensified or weakened, or even ceases altogether. Now one planet acts, now another, now a third and so on. Schematically we can picture these influences in the following way. Imagine a large wheel, hanging upright above the earth, with seven or nine enormous colored spotlights fixed around the rim. The wheel revolves, and the light of now one and now another projector is directed toward the earth. Thus the earth is always colored by the light of the particular projector that illuminates it at a given moment. All beings born on earth are colored by the light prevailing at the moment of birth, and keep this color throughout their lives. No effect can be without cause, and no cause can be without effect. And indeed planets have a tremendous influence both on the life of mankind in general and on the life of every individual person. It is a mistake for modern science not to recognize this influence, even though it is not as great as modern "astrologers" would have us believe.

Always everything influences us, although many influences from the earth, planets and sun cannot reach us if we are wholly under the influence of small things. Every thought, feeling, movement is a result of one or another influence. Everything we do, all our manifestations, are what they are because something influences us from outside. Sometimes this slavery humiliates us, sometimes not. It depends on what we like. On the other hand, we do have some choice, that is, we can keep some influences and free ourselves of others. But we cannot free ourselves from one influence without becoming subject to another. This is why work on oneself ultimately comes down to choosing which influence we will become subject to and actually falling under it. For this, of course, it is necessary to know beforehand which influence is more profitable for us.

To free oneself of chemico-physical influences, one has to be passive. These are the influences that are due to the emanations of the atmosphere of the body, of feeling, of thought, and in some people also of "ether." To be able to resist these influences, we have to be passive. Then we can become a little freer of them. Here the law of attraction operates. Like attracts like, that is, everything goes toward the place where there is more of the same kind. "To him who has much, more is given. From him who has little, even that is taken away." If we are calm, our emanations are heavy, so other emanations come and can be absorbed, as much as we have room for. They occupy empty places where there is a vacuum, and remain where there is calm, where there is no friction. But if we are agitated, we have not enough emanations, for they are going out to others. And if there is no room, if everything is full, emanations may hit against us but they rebound or pass by.

To become free of influences of the second, that is, the associative kind requires an artificial struggle. Here the law of repulsion acts. Where there is more, little can be added, and where little, more is added—that is, it is the reverse of the first law. With influences of this kind everything proceeds according to the law of repulsion.

So in order to free oneself, there are two separate principles for the two different kinds of influences. If we want to be free, we must know which principle to apply in each particular case. If we apply repulsion where attraction is needed, we will be lost. Many of us do the reverse of what is required. But it is easy to discriminate between these two kinds of influences if we take the trouble to look. At first we may not know the difference between emanations and associative impulses. Yet, it is easy to distinguish emanations if we observe them closely, and we can then acquire a taste for discrimination. It is impossible to obtain a result immediately and become free from these influences at once, but study and discrimination are possible for everyone.

To study the associative kind of influence is easier in practice. For instance, take influence through form. People always influence each other through external form, that is, movements, clothes, cleanliness or otherwise—what is generally called the "mask." This influence can easily be changed. As regards the second associative influence, what we have called feeling and relationship, we should know that the attitude of others toward us depends on us, that it often reflects our own attitude. In order to live intelligently, it is important to understand that the responsibility for almost every good or bad feeling lies in ourselves, in our outer and inner attitude. The attitude of other people often reflects our own attitude. Everything is mechanical. We can change our external relationships if we take the necessary measures.

The third kind of influence, suggestion, is very powerful. Every person is under the influence of suggestions, one person suggesting to another. Many suggestions occur very easily, especially if we do not know we are being exposed to suggestion. But even if we do know, suggestions penetrate. It is important to understand that, as a rule, at every moment of our life only one center is working in us—either mind or feeling—and that by itself a center has no consciousness, no critical faculty. Yet it is possible to ensure a critical perception of new material if we take care that, during perception, another center should stand by and perceive the material from aside. This new method consists in the following: when thought is already here, we try to feel, and when we feel something, we try to direct our thought on our feeling. Up to now, thought and feeling have been separated. We begin to watch our mind, to feel what we think. We prepare for tomorrow and safeguard ourselves against deceit.

Every person, according to his individuality, has a limited repertory of postures which are indissolubly connected with distinctive forms of thought and feeling. These forms, which may be called postures of thought and feeling, are so closely bound that we cannot change them without having changed our repertory of moving postures. At the same time, each of our movements, voluntary or involuntary, is an unconscious transition from one automatically fixed posture to another, equally automatic. It is an illusion that our movements are voluntary; in reality they are automatic. Our thoughts and feelings are equally automatic. And the automatism of our thoughts and feelings is definitely connected with the automatism of our movements. One cannot be changed without the other.

A large idea should be taken only with large understanding. For us, small ideas are all we are capable of understanding—if even these. Generally, it is better to have a little thing inside than something big outside. We have to think in a different way than we have thought before.

ACQUIRING A SOUL

A T THE BEGINNING of every religion, we find an affirmation of the existence of God the Word. One teaching says that when the world was still nothing, there were emanations, there was God the Word. God the Word is the world. God said: "Let it be so," and sent the Father and the Son. He is always sending the Father and the Son. And once He sent the Holy Ghost.

Everything in the world obeys the Law of Three. Everything existing came into being in accordance with this law. Combinations of positive and negative principles can produce new results, different from the first and the second, only if a third force comes in. If one person affirms, another denies, but nothing is created until something else is added. Then something new arises.

The Absolute creates in accordance with the same law. Only in this case all the three forces necessary to produce a new manifestation are in the Absolute Himself. He sends them forth from Himself, emanates them. Thereafter the three sometimes change places. The three forces or principles, issuing from the Absolute, have created the whole multitude of suns, one of which is our sun. Each of the suns also emanates, and emanations of the suns, by means of combinations of positive and negative matter, give rise to new formations. The result of one of these combinations is our earth, and the newest combination is our moon. Everything has emanations, and their interaction produces new combinations. This includes man and the microbe.

After the act of creation, existence and emanations go on. Emanations penetrate everywhere according to their possibilities, and thus they also reach man. The result of their interaction is new frictions. The emanations of the sun reach the earth and even go through it unchecked because they are the finest. The emanations of the planets reach the earth but do not reach the sun. The emanations of the earth are still shorter. In this way, within the confines of the earth's atmosphere there are three kinds of emanations—those of the sun, of the earth and of the planets.

The creative activity of the Absolute differs from subsequent acts of creation in that the Absolute creates from Himself. Only the Absolute has Will, and He alone sends forth the three forces from Himself. Subsequent acts of creation proceed mechanically, by means of interaction based on the same Law of Three. No single entity in isolation can create by itself—only collective creation is possible.

The creative activity of the Absolute proceeds toward man in the direction given by the original impulse. In accordance with the Law of Octaves, this development can go on only up to a certain point. In the cosmic ray of creation the line issuing from the Absolute and ending in our moon can be envisioned as like a ladder, with the moon as its base. The main points of this line of creation are: Absolute, sun, earth and the last point, moon. Between these four points there are three octaves: Absolute—sun; sun—earth; and earth—moon. Each of these points is a *do*. Between them, at three points, there are, as it were, three machines whose function is to make *fa* pass into *mi*.

All through the cosmic octave the shock at *fa* must come from outside, and the shock at *si* comes from inside the *do*. By means of these, involution proceeds from top to bottom, and evolution from bottom to top. The life of man plays the same role as the planets in relation to earth, earth in relation to moon, and all suns in relation to our sun. Everything is governed by a law, a very simple law as applied outside. We need to find out how the law works in us. In accordance with it, we can follow either the law of evolution or the law of involution, provided we put the outside law inside.

In our system we are created in the image of God—of a trinity. If we consciously absorb three substances and send them out, we can construct outside ourselves what we like. This is creation. But when this takes place through us it is the creation of the Creator. In this case, all three forces manifest separately in us and combine outside us. Every creation can be either subjective or objective.

To have a soul is the aim of all religions, of all schools. It is only an aim, a possibility—not a fact. A child is never born with a soul, and ordinary man has no soul and no will. There is no master in ordinary man, and if there is no master, there is no soul. A soul can be acquired only in the course of life, and even then it is a great luxury and only for a few. Most people live all their lives without a soul, without a master, and for ordinary life a soul is quite unnecessary.

But a soul cannot be born from nothing. Everything is material and so is the soul, only it consists of very fine matter. Consequently, in order to acquire a soul, it is first of all necessary to have the corresponding matter. Since we do not have enough materials even for our everyday functions, we must begin to economize, so that something may remain. The reserve of substances that must be accumulated has to be large. Otherwise, what there is will soon be dissipated. If, for example, we have some crystals of salt and put them into a glass of water, they will quickly dissolve. More can be added over and over again, and they will still dissolve. But there comes a moment when the solution is saturated. Then the salt no longer dissolves and the crystals remain whole at the bottom. It is the same with the human organism. Even if materials that are required for the formation of a soul are being constantly produced in the organism, they are dispersed and dissolved in it. There must be a surplus of such materials in the organism. Only then is crystallization possible.

The material crystallized after such a surplus takes the form of another body, a copy of the person's physical body, and may be separated from it. Each body has a different life and each is subject to different orders of laws. The new, or second, body is called the "astral" body. In relation to the physical body it is what is called the soul. To build this body inside man is the aim of all religions and all schools. Every religion has its own special way, but the aim is always the same. If the second body becomes crystallized, it can continue to live after the death of the physical body. The matter of this astral body, in its vibrations, corresponds to matter of the sun's emanations and is, theoretically, indestructible within the confines of the earth and its atmosphere.

X

KNOWLEDGE
OF BEING

OBJECTIVE ART

P EOPLE LIVING ON THE EARTH belong to highly disparate levels, even though they look exactly the same in appearance. Just as there are very different levels of people, so there are different levels of art. But the difference between these levels is far greater than we think. We take different things as being on one level, far too near one another, and we assume these different levels are accessible to us.

What we call art is simply mechanical reproduction, imitating nature or other people, or mere fantasy, or striving to be original. Real art is something else entirely. True works of art, especially ancient art, contain elements that are inexplicable, a certain "something" we do not feel in contemporary art. We all sense the difference, but since we do not understand it, we easily forget it and assume that all art is the same. And yet there is an enormous difference between our art and this other art. In our art everything is subjective—the artist's perception of this or that sensation, the forms in which he expresses it, and the perception of these forms by other people. In one and the same subject one artist may feel one thing and another artist a completely different thing. The same sunset, for example, may evoke joy in one artist and sadness in another. Two artists may strive to express identical perceptions by completely different forms and techniques, or completely different perceptions in the same way—each according to his training, which he follows or disregards. And the viewers, listeners or readers will perceive, not what the artist felt or wished to convey, but what the forms he employed will make them feel by association. Every aspect of the artistic process is subjective, and everything is accidental. The artist does not "create"; he occupies himself with a work that "gets created." He is in thrall to thoughts and moods that he himself does not understand and cannot control; they rule him and can express themselves in various ways. Since the work's form is totally accidental, it acts on people accidentally in various ways depending on their mood, tastes, habits, the kind of hypnosis they are under and so on.

In real, objective art there is nothing accidental. Here the artist actually does "create," that is, he makes what he intends, putting into his work whatever ideas and feelings he wants to put into it. This work acts on people in a definite and specific way. They receive precisely what the artist wanted to transmit, although the same work produces different impressions on people of different levels of understanding. This is real, objective art. Imagine some scientific work—for example, a book on astronomy or chemistry. It is impossible for two qualified people to understand it in different ways. Every literate person, with adequate preparation, will understand precisely what the author means to express. An objective work of art is just such a book, except that it affects the emotional as well as the intellectual side of us.

Such works of objective art exist today. The great Sphinx in Egypt is one, and there are many others, including certain historically recognized works of architecture, certain statues of gods. There are divine and mythological figures that can be read like books, not only with the mind but with the emotions, provided they are sufficiently developed. In the course of our travels in Central Asia we found, in the desert at the foot of the Hindu Kush, a strange figure that we assumed was some kind of ancient god or demon. At first we took it as a mere curiosity, but after a while we began to *feel* that this figure contained many things, in fact, a complete and complex system of cosmology. And slowly we began, step by step, to decipher this system. We found it expressed in the body of the figure, in its legs, its arms, its head, its eyes, its ears—it was everywhere. Absolutely nothing in the statue was accidental, nothing was insignificant. And gradually we understood the aim of the people who built the statue, and began to feel their thoughts, their feelings. Some of us even thought that we saw their faces and heard their voices. Regardless, the fact remains that we grasped the meaning of what they wanted to convey across thousands of years, and not only the meaning but all of the feelings and emotions connected with their message. Now *that* was a work of art!

A STREAM OF MYTHS
AND SYMBOLS

O NE OF THE CENTRAL IDEAS of objective knowledge is that of the unity of all things, of unity in diversity. From ancient times people who have understood the content and significance of this idea, and have seen in it the basis of objective knowledge, have endeavored to find a way to transmit it in a form that could be understood by others. Bearers of objective knowledge have always regarded its transmission as their duty. In this transmission, the idea of the unity of all things had to be conveyed first, and as completely and precisely as possible. And to do this the idea had to be put into forms that could be received by others without its being distorted or corrupted. To accomplish this, the people who were to receive the idea had to be properly prepared. The idea itself was then put either into a logical form, as in philosophical systems that endeavor to define the "fundamental principle" from which all phenomena are derived, or into religious creeds that endeavor to inspire faith in order to evoke a wave of emotion raising believers to the level of "objective consciousness." These two ways of conveying the idea of unity run, with greater or lesser success, through the course of human history from earliest antiquity to our own time. Philosophical and religious doctrines remain like monuments along the path tread by those who have attempted to unite esoteric thought and the thought of mankind.

But objective knowledge, including the idea of unity, belongs to objective consciousness. The forms that express it are inevitably distorted when perceived by subjective consciousness and result not in the acquisition of truth but only in greater delusion. Objective consciousness allows one to see and feel the unity of all things, but subjective consciousness divides the world into millions of separate and unconnected phenomena. Attempts to connect these phenomena on a scientific or philosophical basis lead to nothing because we cannot reconstruct the idea of the whole from its scattered remnants, and we cannot determine how it is divided without understanding the laws upon which this division is based.

Nevertheless, the idea of the unity of all things can be found in intellectual thought, but its relation to diversity cannot be accurately represented in words or logical forms. Language always gets in the way. Our language has been designed to express impressions of plurality and diversity received in subjective states of consciousness, and is incapable of fully and comprehensibly transmitting the idea of unity that is intelligible and obvious only in the objective state of consciousness.

Realizing the imperfections and limitations of ordinary language, the people who have possessed objective knowledge have tried to express the idea of unity in "myths," "symbols" and certain "verbal formulas" that, in being transmitted without alteration, have passed on the idea from one school to another, often from one era to another. "Myths" and "symbols" were intended to reach man's higher centers which function in higher states of consciousness. The aim was to transmit ideas inaccessible to the intellect, and to transmit them in such a way that they could not be misinterpreted. "Myths" were intended for the higher feeling center; "symbols" for the higher thinking center. This is why all attempts to understand or explain "myths" and "symbols" with the ordinary mind, or the formulas and the expressions that summarize their content, are doomed from the start. Understanding anything is possible only with the appropriate center. But the preparation for receiving ideas belonging to objective knowledge must proceed on an intellectual basis, for only a mind that is properly prepared can transmit them to the higher centers without introducing foreign elements.

The symbols that were used to transmit ideas belonging to objective knowledge included diagrams of the fundamental laws of the universe, which not only transmitted the knowledge itself but also showed the way to it. The study of symbols, including both their construction and their meaning, formed an important part of the preparation for receiving objective knowledge and itself functioned as a test of the students' potential. If they understood a symbol merely in a literal or formal way, this in and of itself made it impossible to receive any further knowledge. Symbols were divided into two categories. Fundamental symbols included the principles of separate domains of knowledge, and subordinate symbols expressed the essential nature of phenomena in their relation to unity.

One of the formulas summarizing the content of many symbols was particularly important: "As above, so below" from *The Emerald Tablet of Hermes Trismegistus*. This formula states that all of the laws of the cosmos are reflected in all phenomena, from a single atom to any object that exists. This same meaning is contained in the analogy between the *microcosm* and the *macrocosm*—between man and the universe. The fundamental laws of triads and octaves penetrate all things and should be studied simultaneously both in the world and in man. But in relation to himself man is a much more accessible object of study and knowledge than the world of phenomena outside. Therefore, in striving toward knowledge of the universe, we should begin with the study of ourselves and the realization of the fundamental laws within us. From this point of view, there is another dictum, *"Know thyself,"* that is profoundly significant in being one of the formulas that leads to the knowledge of truth. The study of the world and the study of man assist one another. In studying the world and its laws, we also study ourselves, and in studying ourselves we study the world. Every symbol thus teaches us something about ourselves.

The understanding of symbols can be approached in the following way. In studying the phenomenal world, we first of all see two opposing principles manifested in everything. Their various combinations, whether through conjunction or opposition, yield results that include a third principle and reflect the essential nature of the principles which have created them. We can see these great laws of *duality* and *trinity* manifested simultaneously in the cosmos and in ourselves. In relation to the cosmos we are merely spectators, and we see only the surface of phenomena that seem to move in one direction but actually are moving in various directions. In regard to ourselves, on the other hand, the understanding of the laws of duality and trinity can be expressed in a practical form. A person who has understood these laws in himself can, so to speak, direct their manifestation to the permanent line of struggle with himself on the way to self-knowledge. In this way he will introduce the *line of will* first into the circle of time and afterward into the cycle of eternity, which will create in him the great symbol known as the *Seal of Solomon*.

It is impossible to transmit the meaning of symbols to someone who has not reached an understanding of them in himself. This sounds paradoxical, but the meaning of a symbol and the revelation of its essence can only be given to and understood by a person who, so to speak, already knows what the symbol contains. The symbol then becomes for him a synthesis of his knowledge, as well as a means for its expression and transmission, just as it was for the person who constructed it.

SYMBOLOGY AND
SELF-KNOWLEDGE

THE MORE SIMPLE SYMBOLS:

or the numbers 2, 3, 4, 5, and 6 which express them, possess a definite meaning in relation to the inner development of man. They represent the various stages on the path of self-perfection and growth of being.

In our ordinary, natural state, we each exist as a *duality*. We consist entirely of dualities or "pairs of opposites." All our sensations, impressions, feelings, thoughts, can be divided into positive and negative, useful and harmful, necessary and unnecessary, good and bad, pleasant and unpleasant. The centers also function according to this kind of opposition. Thoughts, for example, oppose feelings, and moving impulses oppose the instinctive craving for quiet. All of our perceptions, all of our reactions, our entire lives are experienced according to this duality. But this duality is unstable and the opposing sides tend to alternate. What is victor today is the vanquished tomorrow; what is dominant today is subordinate tomorrow. And all these alternations are equally mechanical, equally independent of our will, and equally incapable of leading us to the attainment of any goal. The understanding of duality in oneself begins with realizing our mechanicalness, and recognizing the difference between what is mechanical and what is conscious.

Before we can realize our mechanicalness, we have first to destroy our false assumptions that even our most mechanical actions are voluntary and conscious, and that we each are unitary and whole. When this self-deception is destroyed and we begin to distinguish the mechanical from the conscious in ourselves, there begins a struggle to realize consciousness in our lives and subordinate the mechanical to the conscious. For this purpose, we begin with efforts, coming from conscious motives, to make a definite *decision* against mechanical processes proceeding according to the law of duality. This creation of a permanent third principle is for man the *transformation of the duality into the trinity.*

By strengthening this decision and constantly applying it to all those events in our lives in which accidental neutralizing "shocks" once caused accidental results, we eventually may develop a permanent line of results that represents the *transformation of the trinity into quaternity.* The next stage, in which the quaternity becomes a quinternity, that is, the *construction of the pentagram,* can have many different levels of significance for us, including the crucial and indubitable one that pertains to the work of centers.

The development of the human machine and the enrichment of being begins with a new functioning of this machine, a new relation among the thinking, feeling, moving, instinctive and sex centers. The overdevelopment of one center at the expense of the others produces an extremely one-sided person and forecloses the possibility of further development. But if a person brings the work of the five centers into harmonious accord, he then "locks the pentagram within him" and becomes a completed example of the physically perfect human being. The harmonious functioning of the five centers allows a union with the higher centers, which introduces the missing principle and brings a direct and permanent connection with objective consciousness and objective knowledge. Then a person becomes the *six-pointed star;* that is, by being locked within a circle of life independent and complete in itself, he is isolated from outside influences or accidental shocks, thereby embodying in himself the *Seal of Solomon*.

This series of symbols—represented by the numbers 2, 3, 4, 5 and 6—can be interpreted as applicable to a single process. But even this interpretation is incomplete. A symbol can never be fully interpreted. It can only be experienced, just as, for example, the idea of *self-knowledge* must be experienced.

This process of individual harmonious development can be examined from the point of view of the Law of Octaves, which gives rise to another system of symbols. In the terms of this law, every completed process is a transition of the note *do* through a series of successive tones to the *do* of the next octave. The seven basic notes of the octave express the Law of Seven, and the addition of the *do* of the next octave, that is to say, the crowning of the process, gives the eighth step. The seven basic notes, together with the two "intervals" and "additional shocks," give nine steps, which total ten with the *do* of the next octave. The tenth and final step represents the end of one cycle and the beginning of another. Thus the process of development represented by the Law of Octaves includes the numbers one through ten. At this point we come to what may be termed the *symbolism of numbers,* which cannot be understood without the Law of Octaves or a clear conception of how octaves are expressed in the *decimal* system, and vice versa.

In Western occult systems there is a method known as "theosophical addition," which defines numbers consisting of two or more digits by the sum of those digits. To people who do not understand the symbolism of numbers, this method of synthesizing numbers seems completely arbitrary and pointless. But for a person who understands and has the key to the unity of all things, theosophical addition is profoundly significant in resolving all diversity into the fundamental laws that govern it and are expressed in the numbers one through ten.

As discussed above, in symbology numbers are connected with specific geometrical figures, and are mutually complementary. In the Kabbalah there is another system of symbols based on letters, as well as one based on words. Combining symbolism by numbers, geometrical figures, letters and words results in a methodology that is complex but more perfect. There are also systems of symbols of magic, alchemy and astrology, as well as the symbology of the Tarot which unites them into one whole.

All of these systems can serve as a means for transmitting the idea of unity. But in the hands of the ignorant, despite one's good intentions, the same symbol becomes an "instrument of delusion." The reason for this lies in the fact that a symbol can never be taken as having a final, specific meaning. In expressing the laws of the unity of endless diversity, a symbol itself possesses an endless number of aspects from which it can be examined, and demands that the viewer be able to see it simultaneously from different perspectives. Once transposed into the words of ordinary language, symbols become ossified. They lose their luster and easily become "their own opposite," confining the meaning within a narrow dogmatic frame that does not allow even the very relative freedom of a logical examination of the subject. The cause lies in literal understanding, in attributing only one meaning to the symbol. The truth is again obscured by a film of delusion, and can be rediscovered only with a tremendous effort of negation. It is well known what delusions have arisen from the symbols of religion, alchemy and particularly magic, when people have taken them literally with only one meaning.

Despite this, a correct understanding of symbols can never lead to dispute. It deepens our knowledge and cannot remain theoretical because it motivates us to strive toward real results, toward the union of knowledge and being, that is, to *doing*. Pure knowledge cannot be transmitted, but the symbols that express it are like a veil that becomes transparent for those who desire and know how to look.

This brings us to the symbolism of speech, although not everyone can understand it. To grasp the inner meaning of what is said depends on the listener's level of development, his state and capacity to make corresponding efforts to understand. Typically, on hearing things that are new for us, instead of making efforts to understand, we begin to dispute or refute them, maintaining contrary opinions that seem correct but actually have nothing to do with the real meaning. In this way, we lose all chance of learning anything new. Before we can understand speech when it becomes symbolical, we must have learned and already know how to listen. Any attempt to literally understand speech that deals with objective knowledge, with the union of diversity and unity, is doomed from the outset and leads in most cases to further delusion.

We have to dwell on this point because the intellectualism of contemporary education teaches people to look for scholastic definitions and logical arguments about everything they hear. Without noticing it, we unconsciously fetter ourselves with a desire for exactitude in areas where exact definitions imply inexactitude in meaning. Thanks to this tendency in our thinking, it often happens that exact knowledge concerning details of something, communicated to a person before he has acquired an understanding of its essential nature, only makes that nature even more difficult for him to understand. This does not mean that there are no exact definitions on the path of true knowledge. On the contrary, it is only there that they exist. These definitions, however, are very different from what we tend to think they are. And if anyone supposes that he can follow the way of self-knowledge guided by an exact knowledge of all the details, or if he expects that such knowledge can be acquired without taking the trouble to assimilate what he has received, then he should first of all understand that what he seeks can only be attained if he makes the necessary efforts himself. No one can ever give us what we do not already have, and no one can do our own work for us. All that anyone else can do for us is to give us the impetus to work. From this perspective, symbolism can provide this kind of impetus if it is properly perceived.

THE ENNEAGRAM

I n accordance with the Law of Octaves, every process on every plane is determined entirely by the law of the structure of the seven-tone scale. In this connection, every note in the scale, if taken on another plane, represents again a whole octave. The "intervals" between *mi* and *fa* and between *si* and *do,* which require an external "shock" for the process to continue, by this very fact connect one process with other processes. From this it follows that the Law of Octaves connects all processes of the universe to one another. For those who know the scales of the passage and the laws that govern the structure of the octave, it can allow an exact cognition of everything, every phenomenon, both in its essential nature and in its relation to other phenomena.

For a synthesis of all knowledge connected with the law of the structure of the octave, there is a certain symbol that takes the form of a circle divided into nine parts, with lines connecting the nine points on its circumference in a specific order. Before moving on to study the symbol itself, it is important to understand certain aspects of the teaching that employs this symbol, as well as how this teaching relates to other systems that employ symbolism to transmit knowledge.

In order to understand the interrelation of these various teachings, we have always to remember that the ways leading to the cognition of unity approach it like the radii of a circle moving toward the center—the closer they come to the center, the closer they are to one another. As a result of this, the theoretical statements that form the basis of one line can sometimes be explained from the perspective of statements of another line, and vice versa. It is therefore sometimes possible to form intermediate lines between two adjacent lines. However, without complete knowledge and understanding of the fundamental lines, such intermediate ways can easily lead to lines becoming mixed, that is, to confusion and error.

Of the principal lines, more or less known, four can be named:

1. The Hebraic
2. The Egyptian
3. The Persian
4. The Hindu

Of the last line, we know only its philosophy, and of the first three, certain parts of their theory. In addition to these, there are two lines known in Europe, namely *theosophy* and so-called *Western occultism*, which have come from a mixture of the fundamental lines. There are grains of truth to be found in both these lines, but since neither embodies complete knowledge, any attempt to realize them in practical terms yields only negative results.

The teaching of the Fourth Way is entirely self-sufficient and independent of the other lines, and has been completely unknown until the present day. Like other lines, it employs the symbolic method, and one of its principal symbols is the above-mentioned figure in the following form:

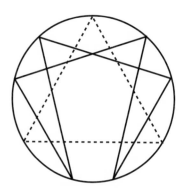

This circle is divided into nine equal parts. It has six points that are connected by a figure which is symmetrical in relation to a diameter passing through the highest point of the divisions of the circumference. This point is the apex of an equilateral triangle linking together the three points of the divisions that do not enter into the construction of the original complex figure. This symbol cannot be found anywhere in the study of "occultism," whether in books or by word of mouth. The people who knew about it considered it so important that they felt it had to be kept secret.

The symbol shown above expresses the Law of Seven in its union with the Law of Three. There are seven notes in the octave, the eighth being a repetition of the first. Together with the two "additional shocks" that fill the "intervals" *mi-fa* and *si-do*, there are nine elements. A complete version of this symbol, which connects it with a complete representation of the Law of Octaves, would be more complex than this one. But this version already shows the inner laws of a *single octave*, and provides us with a method for cognizing the essential nature of any one thing examined in itself.

Any single thing or phenomenon, when examined in isolation, can be represented as a closed circle, that is, an uninterrupted process that eternally repeats itself. The circle symbolizes this process, and the separate points in the division of the circumference symbolize the steps of the process. The symbol as a whole represents *do*, that is, something with an orderly and complete existence. It is a circle—a complete cycle. It is the *zero* of our decimal system, which is written as a closed cycle. The symbol contains within itself everything necessary for its own existence. It is isolated from its surroundings. The succession of stages in the process must be connected with the remaining numbers from 1 to 9. The ninth step fills the "interval" *si-do* and completes the cycle, that is, it closes the circle, which then begins anew at this point. The apex of the triangle closes the duality of its base, making possible its manifestation in the most diverse triangles, just as it multiplies itself infinitely in the line of its base. Every beginning and every end of the cycle is thus situated at the apex of the triangle, at the point where the beginning and the end merge, where the circle is closed, and which sounds as the two *do*'s in the octave in the endlessly flowing cycle. But it is the ninth step that completes one cycle and begins another. This is why the number 9 occupies the highest point of the triangle corresponding to *do,* with the other numbers 1 through 8 occupying the remaining points.

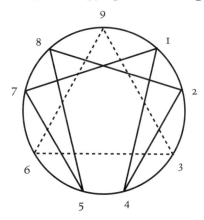

Moving on to the complex figure inside the circle, we should understand the principles of its construction. The laws of unity are reflected in all phenomena, and provide the basis for the numerical decimal system. If we consider a unit as a single note containing a whole octave within itself, then we should divide this unit into seven unequal parts in order to arrive at the seven notes of this octave. But the graphic representation does not take into account the inequality of the parts, and the construction of the diagram takes first one-seventh of the whole, then two-sevenths, three-, four-, five-, six- and seven-sevenths. These divisions can be represented as decimals:

1/7—0.142857 . . .
2/7—0.285714 . . .
3/7—0.428571 . . .
4/7—0.571428 . . .
5/7—0.714285 . . .
6/7—0.857142 . . .
7/7—0.999999 . . .

In examining this list of periodic decimal fractions, we see at once that, in all except the last case, the series after the decimal point consists of exactly the same six digits running in a definite sequence. Therefore, if we know the first digit of a given series, we can reconstruct the whole period in full.

If we now place all the numbers from 1 to 9 on the circumference, and connect those in the period by straight lines according to their order in the period, then, regardless of which such number we start from, we shall obtain the figure found inside the circle. The numbers 3, 6 and 9 are not included in the period, but form a separate triangle—the free trinity of the symbol.

Making use of "theosophical addition" and taking the sum of the numbers of the period, we obtain *nine*, that is, the whole octave. Again, each separate note also includes another whole octave that is subject to the same laws as the first. The arrangement of the notes will correspond to the numbers of the period, and the drawing of an octave will be as follows:

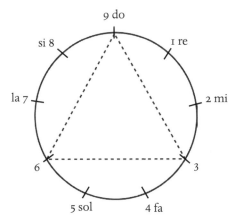

The triangle 9-3-6, which unites the three points on the circumference that are not included in the period, connects together the Law of Seven and the Law of Three. Two of the numbers not included in the period, namely 3 and 6, correspond to the two "intervals" in the octave, while the third is, so to speak, superfluous, although it does replace the fundamental note that is not in the period. Moreover, any phenomenon capable of acting reciprocally with a phenomenon of the same kind sounds as the note *do* in a corresponding octave. Thus, *do* can emerge from its own circle and enter into correlation with another circle, thereby fulfilling the role in another cycle that is played by the "shocks" filling the "intervals" in its own octave. It is thanks to this potential that *do* is connected through the triangle 3-6-9 with those places in the octave where the shocks from outside occur, where the octave can be penetrated and connected with what exists outside it. The Law of Three stands out in relief, so to speak, from the Law of Seven; the triangle penetrates, shines through the period. These two figures in combination represent the inner structure of the octave and its notes.

At this point it would be entirely reasonable to ask why the "interval" designated by the number 3 is where it should be between the notes *mi* and *fa*, while the one designated by the number 6 is located between *sol* and *la* when it should be between *si* and *do*. The placement of the interval apparently in *its wrong place* itself shows to those able to read the symbol the kind of "shock" that is required for the passage of *si* to *do*. In order to understand this, we have to recollect what was said about the role of "shocks" in the processes that take place in man and in the universe.

When we discussed the Law of Octaves as applied to the cosmos, we saw that in the cosmic octave "Absolute—moon" the passage of *do* to *si*, the filling of the interval, is accomplished by the will of the Absolute. The passage *fa-mi* occurs mechanically with the help of a special machine that makes it possible for *fa*, which enters it, to acquire, through a series of inner processes, the characteristics of *sol* standing above it without changing its note. It thus accumulates, as it were, the internal energy for passing independently into *mi*, the next note.

Exactly the same relationship can be found in every completed process. For example, the very same "intervals" and "shocks" can be found in the processes by which the human organism takes in and transforms nutritive substances. As mentioned in chapter II, man takes in three kinds of food. Each one of them is the beginning of a new octave. The second, that is, the air octave, joins up with the first, that is, the octave of food and drink, at the point where the first octave comes to a stop at the note *mi*. And the third octave joins up with the second at the point where the second octave comes to a stop at the note *mi*. This allows development to continue. However, just as in many chemical processes, only definite *quantities* of substances, precisely determined by nature, yield compounds of the required quality, so in the human organism the three kinds of food must be mixed in specific proportions.

The final substance in the process of the food octave is represented as reaching the level *si*, which needs an "additional shock" in order to pass into a new *do*. But as three octaves have participated in the production of this substance, their influence determines the quality of the final result. It is thus possible to control the quality and quantity by regulating the three kinds of food received by the organism. The required result can be obtained only when the three kinds of food have been brought into a state of harmonious conformity by strengthening or weakening the different parts of the process.

But it is essential to remember that no attempts to regulate food or breathing can lead to the desired result unless we know exactly what we are doing, why we are doing it, and what kind of result it will give. And furthermore, even if we were to succeed in regulating two components of the process, that is, our food and breathing, this would not be enough because the most important thing is to regulate the food of "impressions," which enter the upper story of our machine as discussed below. Therefore, before even thinking about practically influencing the inner processes, we must have a precise understanding of the specific relationship between the substances entering the organism, the nature of the possible "shocks," and the laws that govern the transition of notes. These laws are everywhere the same. In studying man we study the cosmos; in studying the cosmos we study man.

The cosmic octave "Absolute—moon" can, according to the Law of Three, be broken into three subordinate octaves. It is in these three octaves that the cosmos is like man—the same three "stories," the same three shocks, where the interval *fa-mi* appears. These points are marked on the diagram, representing "devices" that are found there in the same way as in the human body.

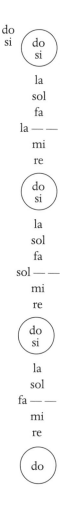

The process of the transition *fa-mi* can be represented schematically as in the diagram. The cosmic *fa* enters the machine like the food of the lower story and begins its cycle of changes. Therefore, in the beginning it sounds in the machine as *do*. The substance *sol* of the cosmic octave enters the middle story like the air in breathing, which in turn helps the note *fa* inside the machine to pass into the note *mi*. This *sol*

on entering the machine also sounds as *do*. The matter that has been obtained is now joined by the substance of the cosmic *la*, which enters the upper story, also as *do*.

As we see from this, the notes *la, sol, fa* serve as food for the machine. According to the Law of Three, the notes in their order of succession will be *la* as the active element, *sol* the neutralizing, and *fa* the passive. When the active relates with the passive with the help of the neutralizing principle, it produces a specific result that can be symbolically represented as in the diagram of the triangle. This symbol indicates that the substance *fa*, in being mixed with the substance *la*, yields as a result the substance *sol*. As this process proceeds in the octave, developing, as it were, inside the note *fa*, it is thus possible to say that *fa* acquires the properties of *sol* without changing its pitch.

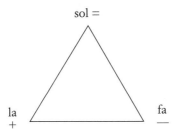

Everything that has been said about the octaves of radiation and the food octaves in the human organism is directly related to the symbol of a circle divided into nine parts. As the expression of a perfect synthesis, this symbol contains within itself all of the elements of the laws it represents, and everything relating to these octaves, and many other things, can be extracted from it and with its help transmitted.

Each completed whole, each cosmos, each organism, *each plant*, is an enneagram, but not every one has an inner triangle. The inner triangle represents the presence of higher elements, according to the scale of materiality, in a given organism. This inner triangle is possessed by plants such as, for example, hemp, poppy, hops, tea, coffee and tobacco, that play a specific role in human life. The study of these plants can teach us many things about the enneagram.

It should be understood that, generally speaking, the enneagram is a *universal symbol*. All knowledge can be included in it, and with its help can be interpreted. This is why we can only claim to *know*, that is, to understand, what we are able to put into the enneagram. Whatever we cannot put into the enneagram we do not truly understand. A person who is able to make use of the enneagram has absolutely no need for books and libraries. *Everything* can be included and read in the enneagram. A person may be all alone in the desert and still trace the enneagram in the sand and read in it the eternal laws of the universe. Every time he can learn something new, something he did not know before.

If two people from different schools meet, they can draw the enneagram and with its help they will be able instantly to determine who knows more and who is on which step, that is, who is the teacher and who the pupil. The enneagram is the fundamental hieroglyph of a universal language that has as many different meanings as there are levels of man.

The enneagram is *perpetuum mobile,* the *perpetual motion* that people have sought in vain since earliest antiquity. The reason is obvious why they could not find it—they looked outside themselves for that which was within them. They tried to construct perpetual motion as a machine is constructed, whereas real perpetual motion is actually part of another perpetual motion and cannot be created apart from it. The enneagram is thus a schematic of perpetual motion, that is, of a machine of eternal movement. But, of course, it can only be read by those who know how to read it. The understanding of this symbol and the ability to make use of it can give a person tremendous power. It is at once perpetual motion as well as the philosopher's stone of the alchemists. The knowledge of the enneagram has been preserved in secret for a very long time. It is now available to all, but only in an incomplete, theoretical form that no one can make use of without instruction from a person who knows.

In order to understand the enneagram it must be thought of as being in motion, as moving. A motionless enneagram is a dead symbol. The living symbol is in motion like everything in life. A motion does not follow a straight line but has simultaneously a twofold direction, circling around itself and falling toward the nearest center of gravity. This law of falling, which is usually called the law of motion, is one of the universal laws known in very ancient times.

As cautioned in the introduction, one should take nothing literally. A large idea should be taken only with large understanding.

Biographical Notes

GEORGE IVANOVITCH GURDJIEFF (1866–1949)

Despite personal accounts and biographies, Gurdjieff, the man, remains the enigma he posed to his closest followers. Jeanne de Salzmann, who worked at his side for thirty years, concluded it was impossible really to know him: "The impression he gave of himself was never the same. . . . You might think you knew Gurdjieff very well, but then he would act quite differently and you would see that you did not really know him." P. D. Ouspensky felt the same: "Among ourselves we often said we never saw him and never would." Gurdjieff did not share details of his personal life, and his autobiographical book, *Meetings with Remarkable Men*, reads less like a historical account than an episodic tale of spiritual adventure.

Gurdjieff was born and raised in the Caucasus mountain region of southern Russia, the son of a Greek father and an Armenian mother. He wrote that he spent his young adult years in search of esoteric knowledge, in expeditions ranging from Greece and Egypt, through the Middle East, to the mountains of the Hindu Kush and Tibet. He did not reveal the sources he investigated, and only spoke vaguely of having been in Christian and Tibetan monasteries, as well as Sufi schools in eastern Persia. Indeed, he disclosed few facts about his journeys and experiences. Nevertheless, he demonstrated both extraordinary resourcefulness in survival and skill in role-playing and disguise, and he was known to have traveled widely through Central Asia, including several trips to Tibet, a country closed to foreign visitors. These activities convinced British Intelligence that he was an undercover agent of the Tsarist government.

Gurdjieff acknowledged that he was not alone in his search but did not identify his comrades. He said only that his mission originated in the early 1890s at the foot of the Egyptian pyramids when he met two older Russians with a kindred obsession about the mystery of human life. In *Meetings with Remarkable Men*, he named the men Prince Yuri Lubovedsky, an erudite and widely traveled spiritual explorer who was his "closest friend," and Professor Skridlov, an archeologist. In undertaking their quest for ancient wisdom, they called themselves the "Seekers of Truth," setting their aim on the ultimate knowledge of reality.

One ardent Russian seeker who visited the pyramids in 1890 was Prince Esper Esperovitch Ukhtomsky (1861–1921). A scholar-diplomat advising the government on non-Christian religions within the Russian Empire, Ukhtomsky traveled widely in Russia and abroad, including countries in Central Asia and the Far East, as well as in Europe. He combined a mystical understanding of Christianity with a deep commitment to Buddhism and Buddhist practice. And he specially admired Madame H. P. Blavatsky,* who asserted that Christianity and other traditional religions were based on a common esoteric doctrine that had originated thousands of years earlier in India, and spread over centuries through Assyria, Egypt, and Greece.

In 1890–1891 Prince Ukhtomsky visited the pyramids with the future Tsar Nicholas II and then proceeded east to India, stopping in Madras at the headquarters site of Blavatsky's Theosophy movement. In his published record of the journey, Ukhtomsky extolled Blavatsky's broad knowledge of religious traditions and endorsed her call for a society of theosophists. He expressed his own vision of the necessity of founding

---

* The co-founder of the Theosophical Society, who published *Isis Unveiled* in 1877 and *The Secret Doctrine* in 1888.

a society "of seekers of Truth in the broadest sense of the word for . . . penetrating deep into the most secret doctrines of Eastern religions." Over the next decade, Ukhtomsky advised the Tsar's foreign affairs and intelligence ministries on Asian diplomacy, including relations with the Dalai Lama in Tibet.

Prince Ukhtomsky's visit to Egypt in 1890 and his idealistic concept "seekers of Truth—together with his title, extensive travels, and profound interest in esoteric religions—all invite the supposition that he was the real-life Prince Lubovedsky, the senior member of the Seekers of Truth. If so, then Gurdjieff, in carrying out missions in Tibet and other countries on Ukhtomsky's authority, would have—as British Intelligence suspected—in fact been acting as an agent of the Tsarist government. In addition, Ukhtomsky and Gurdjieff together would have decided on the form of the teaching and their plan to introduce it to the West, first by recruiting Ouspensky to promote the Fourth Way, and eventually by creating an organization for its practice.

In 1912 Gurdjieff began to gather followers in Moscow and in 1915, after recruiting Ouspensky, formed a study group in St. Petersburg. Ouspensky described his impression of Gurdjieff as follows:

One was struck by a great inner simplicity and naturalness in him which made one completely forget that he was, for us, the representative of the world of the miraculous and the unknown. Furthermore, one felt very strongly in him the entire absence of any kind of affectation or desire to produce an impression. And together with this one felt an absence of personal interest in anything he was doing, a complete indifference to ease and comfort and a capacity for not sparing himself in work whatever that work might be. . . . He was an extraordinarily versatile man; he knew everything and could do everything.

In assimilating the teaching over a period of eighteen months, Ouspensky was amazed at Gurdjieff's speed in transmitting the ideas, his "astonishing capacity for bringing into prominence all principal and essential points and not going into unnecessary details until the principal points had been understood." Ouspensky did not know whether Gurdjieff had prepared his presentation with his fellow Seekers of Truth or with his Moscow group.

In 1917, to escape the violence of the Russian Revolution, Gurdjieff moved to the Caucasus and spent the summer in Essentuki with Ouspensky and a dozen members of the Russian groups. In this communal life he introduced methods of practical self-study, and unfolded what Ouspensky called the "plan of the whole work," including the organization of "schools." In *Meetings with Remarkable Men*, Gurdjieff wrote that while in Essentuki he and Professor Skridlov made a last climb together to a mountain summit surveying Mount Elbrus and a panorama of extraordinary beauty. Having already bidden farewell to Prince Lubovedsky, both men knew that this was the final reunion of the Seekers of Truth. From then on, with Russia sliding inexorably into chaos, Gurdjieff would be alone in carrying out their aim to bring the Fourth Way to the West.

At the end of the summer of 1917, Gurdjieff, suddenly and without explanation, announced that he was stopping all work and dispersed the group. While Ouspensky stayed behind in Essentuki, Gurdjieff moved on with a handful of remaining followers, avoiding conflicting armies, and eventually arrived at Tiflis in early 1919. There he met Alexandre de Salzmann, a well-known Russian painter and stage designer, and his wife, Jeanne, a teacher of music and dance. She described her experience as follows:

> The first impression of Gurdjieff was very strong, unforgettable. He had an expression I had never seen, and an intelligence, a force, that was different, not the usual intelligence of the thinking mind but a vision that could see everything. He was, at the same time, both kind and very, very demanding. You felt he would see you and show you what you were in a way you would never forget in your whole life.

In Tiflis Gurdjieff first established the Institute for the Harmonious Development of Man, which featured his dance exercises called the Movements, based on Tibetan and dervish rituals he had witnessed. Yet, once again, political instability forced him and his followers, now including the de Salzmanns, to emigrate in 1920 to Constantinople. There, he reopened the Institute, only to close it the following year and again move on, this time to Western Europe. He eventually settled in France in 1922, reopening the Institute for the last time at the Château du Prieuré near Fontainebleau outside Paris.

It was at the Prieuré that Gurdjieff achieved widespread recognition, largely from public demonstrations of the Movements. There were sixty to seventy residents, around half of whom were Russian émigrés, who were joined by visitors on weekends. Activities centered on manual labor, principally maintenance and construction, as well as work on the dance exercises. Gurdjieff assigned responsibilities to each person and supervised all the details. In late 1923 he held a Movements demonstration at the prestigious Théâtre des Champs-Elysées in Paris, and in the spring of 1924 visited the United States to give demonstrations in New York at Carnegie Hall and in other major cities. His avowed aim was to establish a branch of the Institute in New York.

After returning to France, Gurdjieff suffered a near-fatal automobile accident and closed the Institute. For the next ten years, he turned all his energies to writing his trilogy on the life of man, titled *All and Everything*. He stopped writing in 1935 and thereafter gave himself to intensive work with selected pupils in Paris until his death in 1949.

In his later years Gurdjieff regarded the study of the original system of ideas as merely a preliminary stage of the work toward consciousness. He turned aside questions about ideas as being theoretical and brought his teaching in terms of a direct perception of reality. Toward the end of his life, he returned to the practice of the Movements and introduced a whole body of dance exercises.

As a spiritual leader, Gurdjieff presented a constant challenge to his followers, making outrageous demands that shocked them and outside observers. According to Ouspensky, "One could be sure of nothing in regard to him. He might say one thing today and something altogether different tomorrow." For Mme. de Salzmann, he was a spiritual "master" in the traditional sense—not as a teacher of doctrine but one who by his very presence awakened and helped others in their search for consciousness. But, she said, he was largely misunderstood in his behavior and methods. On the one hand, by his guidance and presence, he helped followers open to a moment of truth, of reality in themselves, and drew them toward him, toward another level of being. At the same time, he played a role that made them see their actual state, with relentless pressure and shocks, pushing them to extreme limits and forcing them to react against him. This he did without mercy, obliging followers to come to a decision, to face what they really wanted for themselves. As she wrote,

> Here was the grandeur of Gurdjieff. The first way, work on our essence, was outside life, wholly concentrated on inner action. The second, work on our functions, was in life itself and through life. With one hand he called us; with the other he beat us, showing us our slavery to our functions. Very few people had the chance to experience both sides. Yet it is impossible to understand Gurdjieff's methods or behavior without having received material of both these aspects of his work.

Although magnetically charismatic, Gurdjieff did not allow the dependence or adulation often inspired by spiritual leaders, and constantly pushed his followers to come to their own initiative. In fact, he made them leave to pursue their own lives when he deemed it necessary for them or for his larger aims. By disbanding the group in Essentuki and closing his Institute at the Prieuré, he forced a wholesale exodus. By provocation, disregard or simply not making a place for them, he made individual followers come to their own decision to leave.

In introducing the Fourth Way, Gurdjieff was categorical in saying that a person cannot awaken alone, that one must find a leader and others who wish to go in the same direction. For this, a "school" and a group are imperative, at least in the beginning. At the same time, Gurdjieff said that on the Fourth Way there are no permanent forms, and he did not himself try to establish a permanent institution. In building the Prieuré, he remarked, "This is only temporary. In a very short time everything will be different. Everyone will be elsewhere." And in the spring of 1924, after publicly demonstrating the Movements in New York, he confided to Mme. de Salzmann that it would take decades to prepare followers to do the dances as they should be done: "a long time of work—a very long time." When he closed the Institute months later, he in effect abandoned his original proposal to lead an organization with a large number of pupils.

One of the most striking features of Gurdjieff's teaching is the sense of cosmic scale and of history, referring back to ancient civilizations thousands of years ago. With this perspective, including the early history of Christianity, he knew that this appearance of the Fourth Way would be a process drawn out over generations. The Seekers of Truth had rediscovered the ancient science of man's relation to the universe, and Gurdjieff had transmitted the system in talks and his own books. In organizing his Institute, he had also indicated that the Fourth Way involved more than studying the ideas, that an esoteric teaching required practical work for self-knowledge and an engagement with others. Yet in order to appear on a larger scale, the teaching had to be disseminated to a much broader audience, and the forms of practical work had to be demonstrated by establishing an actual "school." Meeting these conditions depended on Gurdjieff's two closest followers, as outlined in the succeeding biographical notes.

All and Everything was published in three series as *Beelzebub's Tales to His Grandson* (1950), *Meetings with Remarkable Men* (1963), and *Life Is Real Only Then, When "I Am"* (1975). The system of ideas brought from 1915 to 1924 was published in Ouspensky's *In Search of the Miraculous: Fragments of an Unknown Teaching* (1949) and in *Views from the Real World* (1973). Gurdjieff's later teaching on the direct perception of reality was reconstructed in Mme. de Salzmann's book *The Reality of Being: The Fourth Way of Gurdjieff* (2010).

Peter Demianovitch Ouspensky (1878–1947)

The Seekers of Truth reconstructed the ancient teaching for perceiving reality, which Gurdjieff undertook to transmit. He, however, was an unknown adventurer from a remote part of Russia who, speaking incorrect Russian with a Caucasian accent, could not command an audience in Russia or Western Europe. It was therefore Ouspensky who played the leading role in promoting the Fourth Way and who, more than any other person, attracted followers to the teaching. Boris Mouravieff, a contemporary Russian émigré who knew both men, observed, "One can say, without exaggeration, that without Ouspensky, Gurdjieff's career in the West would probably not have gone beyond the stage of endless conversations in cafés."

Ouspensky was born in Moscow into a family of the Russian intelligentsia. A precocious child, he began reading at the age of five and by fifteen he had left school. Three years later he started writing and gave up trying to obtain a university degree. Although he had a keen intellect, he was essentially a romantic in his view of the universe and human spirituality. Distrusting all forms of academic science, he felt professors were killing science in the same way priests were killing religion.

From 1896 to 1905 Ouspensky attended various Russian and European universities, and then became a journalist. Like many Russian intellectuals of that time, he was profoundly disillusioned with the aimless routine of life. He began his own search for the miraculous in occult literature, particularly Theosophy. This included experiments in altered states of consciousness, which convinced him of a reality behind the mirage of the visible world.

In 1912 Ouspensky published *Tertium Organum* in Russian, which asserted that accepted patterns of thinking, created by contemporary science, had limited human consciousness to the world of positivist phenomena, cutting man off from the noumenal world and the experience of reality. The following year he set off on a journey to the East, seeking a "school" of esoteric knowledge. Like Prince Ukhtomsky almost twenty years before, he visited Mme. Blavatsky's Theosophy center in India. He spent over a year in that country before abandoning his quest at the outbreak of the first world war and returning to Russia.

In 1915 Ouspensky was introduced to Gurdjieff and helped him form a study group in St. Petersburg. Over some eighteen months, Gurdjieff revealed to the group the structure of an unknown science, which the group called the "System." In 1917 Ouspensky and other members of the group went with Gurdjieff to Essentuki, where Gurdjieff revealed the whole plan of work for practicing the System. After the group was dispersed, Ouspensky made his separate way to Constantinople in early 1920 where, on his own, he held lectures on the Fourth Way. When Gurdjieff arrived six months later, Ouspensky handed over his audience to help Gurdjieff organize his Institute. The following year Ouspensky went to London, where he again gave lectures. When Gurdjieff came to London in 1922, Ouspensky again introduced him to those attending the lectures, after which Ouspensky's followers provided Gurdjieff with the funds to purchase the Château du Prieuré outside Paris. When Gurdjieff reopened his Institute, a number of them sent money and went to work with him. Ouspensky himself visited the Prieuré often during 1923.

In early 1924, Ouspensky decided to separate and work independently from Gurdjieff. He wrote later that he did not understand the direction of Gurdjieff's work and could envision no place for himself in it. Gurdjieff seemed no longer interested in self-study based on ideas, and Ouspensky felt he was accepting pupils who were not intellectually prepared. At the same time, although many observers assumed otherwise, there was no hostility between the two men. Ouspensky did not pretend to be on the same level of understanding, and spoke of his former teacher with great respect and affection. Most important, he had no quarrel with the teaching itself, no disagreement over interpreting the ideas. Thus his choosing to work independently was to end the leader-follower relationship, not to abandon their larger, common aim of promoting the Fourth Way. Nonetheless, because of this decision, he was, then and later, accused of betraying his teacher.

For the remaining 1920s Ouspensky's activities involved private groups, which in the 1930s were expanded by public lectures that eventually attracted hundreds of people. His book *A New Model of the Universe,* which appeared in 1931, popularized his idea of higher dimensions and work on self-study. His lectures on the System, under the title *The Psychology of Man's Possible Evolution,* provided the basis for group meetings in which he answered questions and brought new material. These were supplemented by practical self-study on weekends at country houses of his wife, Mme. Sophie Grigorievna Ouspensky. With the outbreak of World War II, the Ouspenskys emigrated to the United States where, on a much smaller scale, he continued his lectures in New York and she, though bedridden, maintained a country house for work on weekends.

In early 1947, Ouspensky returned to London, urged by followers to reinstitute the lectures suspended by the war. He was, however, in failing health, and knew he had little time to live. In six meetings over a six-month period, he systematically rebuffed questions, and then announced that he had no more help to give. He denied the System as itself a means to attain higher consciousness, effectively foreclosing would-be successors from continuing his work. He died in October 1947.

A year after Ouspensky's death, John Bennett, one of his senior followers, visited Paris to meet with Gurdjieff and determine how to continue the work in England. He was surprised to find Gurdjieff bringing a wholly different teaching, turning away theoretical questions and speaking only in terms of a direct perception of reality. Bennett wrote of his visit: "No one even uses any of the language of the System. It is as if it belongs to the kindergarten and one must not use it in the 'school for big children.'"

Viewed from a historical perspective, Ouspensky's meeting and work with Gurdjieff was critical to the appearance of the Fourth Way. As a writer and lecturer, he was the ideal recruit to receive and promote the teaching. He played a key role in assembling the St. Petersburg group, which provided a forum for Gurdjieff's exposition. Then, in 1921–1922, after *Tertium Organum* in English translation attracted readers in New

York and London, Ouspensky's lectures produced the followers and financial support that allowed Gurdjieff to establish his Institute outside Paris.

When Gurdjieff closed the Institute in 1924, Ouspensky was the only other person capable of independently teaching the Fourth Way. He alone grasped the range of the ideas and the principles of self-study. His assuming this responsibility was critical to sustaining the interest generated by the Institute. After Gurdjieff withdrew and declined to take on pupils, Ouspensky's was the leading public voice for the Fourth Way. The increased interest in the teaching in the 1930s was due to his lectures and meetings. His published account of work with Gurdjieff in *In Search of the Miraculous* attracted readers all over the world for decades after its publication in 1949.

Ouspensky's decision to separate from Gurdjieff was driven by his commitment to the Fourth Way. From the outset, he understood that Gurdjieff's mission was to introduce the teaching for humanity, and that he himself had been recruited to record and transmit the ideas to others. Over time, he came to realize that he would have to promote the teaching independently if he was to fulfill this role. By 1921, when he left Constantinople for London, it was understood that the two men would separate and go to different countries; and he had resolved to resettle in Paris or America if Gurdjieff opened his Institute in London. Three years later, after his followers had been drawn to the Prieuré, Ouspensky concluded that an independent work would be unsustainable unless the separation were definitive. It was then that he announced that his work would proceed "quite independently in the way it had been begun in London in 1921," and prohibited his followers from referring to Gurdjieff or having any relation with others who worked with him.

As outlined in the first section of these notes, Gurdjieff was constantly pressuring followers to come to their own initiative in their lives. It is therefore quite possible, even likely, that he approved of Ouspensky's separation, and may even have suggested it himself. In any event, although, as is well known, both men outwardly appeared incompatible, the break between them was not the rupture presented to their respective followers. Until 1931 they met privately in Paris and Fontainebleau, and afterward Gurdjieff sent Mme. Ouspensky to England to support her husband and maintained contact through Jeanne de Salzmann, Gurdjieff's closest follower. In 1947, immediately after Ouspensky's return to England, Mme. de Salzmann came from Paris to discuss his plans and arrange a last reunion in Gurdjieff's waning years. Although too ill to go to Paris, Ouspensky gave her a present for his former teacher—the manuscript of *Fragments of an Unknown Teaching,* which he had kept private for over twenty years. She returned to France and handed it to Gurdjieff. She said later that, after staying up all night reading the account, Gurdjieff appeared the next morning, deeply moved by the honesty and dedication of his former pupil. It was afterward that Gurdjieff, who alone understood the immensity of Ouspensky's achievement and how it expressed his commitment to the teaching, made the extraordinary statement that he loved Ouspensky.

Gurdjieff condemned followers who independently taught his ideas as "Judas Iscariots." At the time, this sounded like the ultimate charge of betrayal. Almost no one knew that, in fact, Gurdjieff regarded Judas as Christ's closest and most faithful follower, the disciple who selflessly assumed a traitor's role in order to allow his master to fulfill his mission. The "Judas" label was undoubtedly meant for Ouspensky, who, more than any other follower, understood the teaching and Gurdjieff's mission to introduce it. Ouspensky subordinated his personal success, first in providing followers and funds in 1922 to establish Gurdjieff's Institute, then in delaying making his lectures public until 1930 when he could envision no possibility of reopening the Institute, and finally in 1947 in dispersing his independent organization once he learned that Gurdjieff wanted to reunite the senior followers. Ouspensky also bore the condemnation of those who believed he had betrayed his teacher.

In carrying out his independent work, Ouspensky did not pretend to have Gurdjieff's understanding. He took no credit as the source of the teaching, acknowledging that the System originated with a group in Russia. In his lectures and answers, which replicated the format of the St. Petersburg group, he was scrupulously faithful to what he had received. The material was enriched by his own insights but always without distortion. He emphasized that work on oneself should begin with the mind, and he presented the System as the basis for self-study. Nevertheless, having been introduced to practical work in Essentuki in 1917, he repeatedly warned that without it one would "only be learning words," that esoteric ideas which are not taken practically become "mere philosophy—simply intellectual gymnastics that can lead nowhere."

Ouspensky recognized that a change in being required organized work in a "school," a term that, he admitted, should not be applied to his collective study. The System was only an introduction to the Fourth Way. As an introduction, however, his work in London and New York, and particularly *In Search of the Miraculous,* fulfilled his fundamental purpose and established the teaching as a recognized line of psychology. Many of his followers gravitated to Gurdjieff, and after his death continued under Mme. de Salzmann in her organization for practical work on the Fourth Way.

Ouspensky's principal writings include *Tertium Organum* (1912), *A New Model of the Universe* (1931), *The Psychology of Man's Possible Evolution* (1947) and *In Search of the Miraculous* (1949). A record of his talks and answers from 1921–46 was published as *The Fourth Way* (1957).

JEANNE DE SALZMANN (1889–1990)

Gurdjieff was not a prophet, and the Fourth Way is not revealed doctrine to be taken on faith. It is a path to be followed, a practical way to consciousness of reality in oneself. To follow this path requires an individual engagement in self-study, and a collective practice with others based on the principles of the Fourth Way. It was to Jeanne de Salzmann, working with him for thirty years, that Gurdjieff transmitted the practical teaching and these principles, including those for practicing the dance exercises called the Movements. Before he died, he charged her to live another forty years and to do "everything possible—even impossible—in order that what I brought will have an action."

Jeanne de Salzmann was born in Reims, France, the eldest of five children of Jules Allemand and Marie-Louise Matignon, both descendants of old French families. She was brought up in Geneva, Switzerland, in a home strongly influenced by the interaction of her father's Protestant faith and her mother's devout Catholicism, which created a compelling need to understand the truth underlying their Christian belief. Her education was concentrated on music, for which she showed an exceptional gift as a child prodigy. During this period the Conservatory of Geneva included famous musicians from other countries, notably Emile Jacques-Dalcroze, an innovator widely acclaimed for his work in composition, improvisation and dance. At the age of seventeen, Jeanne was chosen, together with a handful of other gifted students, to follow him to the newly completed Dalcroze Institute at Hellerau near Dresden, Germany, and give demonstrations of his work in capitals throughout Europe. It was during her years with Dalcroze that Jeanne met Alexandre de Salzmann, a well-known Russian painter who was assisting Dalcroze in staging and lighting his demonstrations. She married de Salzmann in Geneva in 1911 and returned to his home in Tiflis in the Caucasus where she began her own school of music based on the Dalcroze method.

In 1919, Gurdjieff arrived in Tiflis with a small group of followers, including the composer Thomas de Hartmann. It was through de Hartmann that the de Salzmanns met Gurdjieff, an encounter that was to change the course of their lives. In Gurdjieff and his teaching, Jeanne de Salzmann found the way toward the truth she had longed for since her childhood. When Gurdjieff left Tiflis, the de Salzmanns joined his followers, traveling first to Constantinople and finally settling in Fontainebleau near Paris in 1922. Jeanne de Salzmann remained close to Gurdjieff and worked at his side until his death. She was among the handful of his pupils included in what he called "special work" for a direct perception of reality through conscious sensation.

Before he died, Gurdjieff left Mme. de Salzmann all his rights with respect to his writings and the Movements. At the time, Gurdjieff's followers were scattered across Europe and America. Mme. de Salzmann's first task was to call them to work together. The second was to give the teaching a form for practical work toward consciousness. In the ensuing forty years she arranged for publication of his books and preservation of the Movements. She also established Gurdjieff centers in Paris, New York and London, as well as Caracas, Venezuela.

Gurdjieff was categorical in saying that a person cannot awaken alone, that one must work with others in what he called a "school." Jeanne de Salzmann regarded this condition as absolutely necessary to escape from the narrow circle of ordinary thoughts and feelings. To become conscious of oneself, a person must work with others of comparable experience, who are capable of upending the false scale of values established by personality. It is, however, important to recognize that the term "school" refers to a collective practice, not an institution for acquiring conceptual knowledge. The centers Mme. de Salzmann organized are not exclusive and there are no formal admission requirements or grades of achievement. Indeed, there are no teachers. For a certain time, participants work with a guide who responds to questions. Later, they exchange among themselves. The Fourth Way is a way of understanding, not one of faith or obedience to a charismatic leader.

Toward the end of his life, Gurdjieff openly recognized Jeanne de Salzmann as his closest disciple, telling his followers, "I have entrusted the continuation of my work to her." Yet what he intended only she knew. He had not reopened the Institute closed in 1924, and had only alluded to possibly organizing branches in cities in Europe and America. Nonetheless, in his last two years he encouraged American and English followers to visit him in Paris, and, perhaps more significantly, introduced more than one hundred dance exercises to improvised classes in Paris and New York. The scale of the endeavor suggests a definite aim for the future, which he must have discussed with her. In fact, the speed with which she organized Gurdjieff centers within two years of his death suggests a predetermined plan.

In continuing Gurdjieff's work, Mme. de Salzmann followed his example in refusing to entertain theoretical questions or encourage intellectual discussion of ideas. Her constant demand was for a conscious struggle to be present, although the emphasis changed over time. From a practical study of ordinary functioning, the search deepened in order to discover how to open to reality in oneself. This included working on the relation between the mind and the body, and the experience of a more conscious sensation of presence. Mme. de Salzmann placed importance on coming to this reality in daily meditation, as recommended by Gurdjieff at the beginning of *Beelzebub's Tales*. For advanced followers, she called for opening to a state of unity by experiencing a sense of presence as a second body with its own life.

The core practice established by Mme. de Salzmann is exchange in a group. The exchange may revolve around a specific line of work, theme or text, but it is always a sharing of experiences and questions about the inner work—not a discussion of ideas. In speaking and listening, the constant effort is to be present in order to open to the unknown, an effort toward a possibility of consciousness.

The work in groups is complemented by the practice of Movements, dance exercises that call for a total attention coming from the mind, body and feeling—in effect, the experience of presence in movement. Performing them with one's ordinary attention serves no purpose and, in fact, reinforces one's automatism. This is why, in centers following the Fourth Way, the practice of Movements is strictly limited to participants who are engaged in the group work for consciousness.

The third collective practice instituted by Mme. de Salzmann is sitting meditation, an extension of Gurdjieff's "special work" for a direct perception of reality. Although introduced as a guided work for conscious sensation, after her death these "sittings" were expanded to be occasions for coming together to share the stillness of a more quiet state. Sittings for more advanced participants are often totally silent, while those for newer followers include indications of how to work to be present.

It is important to note that the centers Mme. de Salzmann created were never intended to claim primacy or exclusivity in following the Fourth Way. She said that each center is a "house of work" for change in being, like a school based on the principles of the Fourth Way. Depending on its participants, a house may serve for reaching the level of man number four with a new center of gravity, as well as that of man number five with an indivisible "I." The role of a house in the larger Work depends on the level of its members, although this is beyond ordinary perception because, as Gurdjieff noted, it is not possible to see above one's own level.

In charging her to carry on his work, Gurdjieff instructed Mme. de Salzmann to write down what she brought, which she did, in notebooks, kept like diaries over a forty-year period. This material was published posthumously in her book *The Reality of Being: The Fourth Way of Gurdjieff* (2010).

Mme. de Salzmann died at the age of 101 in Paris in 1990. The centers she created have maintained their collective work along the lines she indicated, and Gurdjieff's teaching of the Fourth Way continues to spread in groups throughout the world.

Fourth Way Centers

The Fourth Way centers organized by Mme. de Salzmann are:

The Gurdjieff Foundation, New York
The Gurdjieff Society, London
L'Institut Gurdjieff, Paris
Fundacion G. I. Gurdjieff, Caracas, Venezuela

For further information, visit www.InSearchofBeing.org.

Index